Because They Matter...

For my dear Rick,
Thank you for so many
years of friendship &
support. I will always
love you! Cindy Traisi
April 1997

By Cindy Traisi

with cover art and illustrations by Dorothy Mushet

First Edition
Library of Congress Catalog Number: 97-90105
Printed in the United States of America

ISBN 0-9656562-0-9

Dedication

For Chuck and Cleveland,
the bravest and the best,

and in memory of my teachers
Sunny, Damian, Nuka, Ria, Treetop,
Tarra and Lucky

Acknowledgments

*To my husband, Chuck, and my boss,
Cleveland Amory—my deepest thanks for giving
me this life and for your trust in me.*

*To Michelle Lyons, Roberta Nau, Barbara Woodhill
and my mother, Dot Fisher—thank you for
making me write this book.*

*To every paid and unpaid staff member past
and present—my deepest thanks.*

*To Dorothy Mushet for the beautiful artwork—
thanks for making my stories have a soul.*

*To Shaun Doole, my harried copy editor and friend—bless
you for telling me how much you enjoyed the manuscript.*

To Dusty, who appointed himself laptop editor in chief.

*To every animal I have ever known, I am the most grateful.
I have learned courage, fear, joy, sadness, the worth of
precious freedom and the kindness of death.
From you I learned humanity.*

Preface

My husband, Chuck, and I are the resident managers of a large wildlife rehabilitation center in Ramona, California, northeast of San Diego in the mountains. The center is owned by the Fund for Animals, Inc., founded by Cleveland Amory—no stranger to people who read good books or to those who love animals—who is our boss.

For more than ten years we have cared for ill, injured or orphaned native wildlife. We have made ourselves available twenty-four hours a day, seven days a week, for emergencies involving wildlife. We have cared for them and treated their injuries or illnesses with great diligence. We have set them free with unimaginable joy in their hearts and ours. We have also watched the light leave their eyes in death. The stories in this book reflect only a few of the thousands of animals that have come to us. Some of these stories are happy and some are sad, but all are meant to give insight into a world that too few of us are able to witness.

How Chuck and I came to follow this road not often taken is a long story. Why we are here—and hopefully always will be—is easy:

Because They Matter . . .

Cindy Traisi

Table of Contents

Wak-Waa   1

Longshot   15

Rasputin   19

Terry   25

Old 2.5   33

Señora Possum   37

Bad Bob   43

"Can-Do" Michelle   51

Bobby and Sugar   69

The Red-Tail with an Attitude   77

Leaping Lena   87

Beakers and Finchie-poo   93

The Egg   99

Baby Bob   103

The Deck Ducks   111

Brave   121

Path   127

"The Thing"   133

Sumo   137

Eggward, the Party Balloons
        and the Last Straw   143

Dog Bite   149

Our Golden Girl   153

Coati-Boy   163

The Night Cranks   169

The Brave Mother   175

Crow   179

Pansy   187

Woody Wood Rat   191

Blacky Raccoon   197

From Grrr to Grover—
        A Tale of Two Possums   205

Ehan   211

Wak-Waa

My husband, Chuck, has a mistress.

I've known it for several years. He knows that I know, and we spend many hours discussing their relationship and laughing at the silly things she does. She is a shameless flirt and hussy who doesn't care whether I'm around during her trysts with Chuck. She has her own home, which Chuck frequents every evening prior to coming to our home.

The "she" in question is a raven. Actually, we do not know whether "she" is a male or a female. We do know, however, that she/he/it is totally devoted to Chuck and that he is equally devoted to her/him/it.

Wak-Waa came to us some years ago, courtesy of our California Fish and Game Department. She had been the illegal "pet" of someone (probably a man) and was confiscated by our local warden. We knew nothing about this bird when she came to us, other than the fact that she had been a "pet." We have had pretty good success in the past at rehabilitating confiscated crows and ravens and releasing them into the wild, so this raven, we thought, was going to be just another rerun.

Our first step in the rehab process was to keep her in the medical center for a few days and give her a good physical exam. We had to be sure she was physically able to be released and could and *would* eat the things she should be eating. Being scavengers, ravens are not hard to please, but sometimes the tamed ones have a hard time adjusting to the totally new environment and have a loss of appetite. This raven suffered from none of the above, so she was a model client and soon was ready for the outdoor flight enclosure. Her wings had been clipped, and since it was January, we knew she would be with us at least until the molt in the spring. In the meantime, at least she could get some exercise and build up her atrophied muscles.

Another step in the rehab process is to minimize human contact and, whenever possible, maximize contact with the same species. While in the medical center and later in the outdoor flight enclosure, we treated this raven as if she were a regular wild animal. We cleaned her cage, fed her and avoided making eye contact. Wak-Waa (the origin of her name comes later) didn't seem to give a rip that we ignored her. In fact, she didn't seem tame or imprinted at all. The only times she appeared slightly aberrant were when other ravens were introduced to her in the flight enclosure. A couple of passing-through ravens with minor injuries were allowed to stay but were totally ignored by Wak-Waa; another few were viciously attacked and had to be immediately removed and placed elsewhere. In any situation with other ravens, it was obvious that this bird didn't have a clue as to what she was.

At that time, except for Chuck, we were an all-female operation. We women were the only people Wak-Waa saw daily except for a few seconds in the late afternoon when Chuck would put in a little extra food for her.

Wak-Waa was in our flight enclosure for months and generally behaved herself—as well as a raven can. She was extremely quiet for a raven, but we felt she was a pretty good candidate for release after she molted those clipped feathers. Our first inclination that we were dealing with a nut case came late one spring morning while we were all scattered about doing various chores. I was filling up water tubs and food dishes that we keep in a secluded area of the property for visiting crows, squirrels, ravens, etc. I was lost in dreamland in the cool canopy of honey locust trees, mindlessly redoing the water tubs, when out of nowhere some man yelled a two-word expletive that one might say to someone they really hated who had made them really mad. I jumped back, squirted myself with the stupid hose and looked around for an irate man storming the property.

There was no one around. I looked in all of the wildlife enclosures around me. I knew the coyote on the hilltop enclosure couldn't speak, and neither could the pigeons in their aviary. I looked over my left shoulder at Wak-Waa alone in her flight cage. My scalp began to prickle as if I'd entered the twilight zone, and an eerie feeling swept over me. Wak-Waa looked at me, hunched her shoulders and said it again.

I freaked and ran to tell everyone that our raven had spoken. Some of our staff had heard the foul language from the opposite end of the property and were amazed to discover that it was from the raven.

The vocalization was extremely human-sounding and unfortunately very intelligible—there was no mistaking what she had said. As it turned out, our raven had a total of three vocalizations: the one previously mentioned; another human-voiced but indecipherable "wak-waa," hence her name; and a third, which I refer to as her "monkey noise"—a series of short "hoo, hoo, hoos," which she generally spoke prior to going into her attack mode, which she did, and still does, on a frequent basis.

Once Wak-Waa rediscovered her vocal cords, things got a little weird around here. Until we moved her outdoors, she apparently had no need to speak, but once in the aviary, she wouldn't shut up, and her favorite words obviously were the expletives.

We found ourselves apologizing to visitors, who completely understood once we related Wak-Waa's story. But still it was bad P.R., and we cringed every time the little dingbat hunched her shoulders to speak. Still, at this point, although she was speaking, Wak-Waa showed no real interest in human companionship.

By summer she had molted, and we could no longer justify keeping her incarcerated. She was strong, healthy, gorgeous and able to fly. She didn't seem to care for humans but still had a mouth (or beak) like a drunken sailor. We hacked (slow reintroduction back to native habitat) her out slowly, simply by opening the aviary door one day and walking away. We kept food in the enclosure and made no effort to hurry her out. Freedom was apparently something she had never known, and she seemed totally bewildered by it all.

She spoke more on that day than I had ever heard her speak before. I think she was nervous and talking just to calm herself. She made a couple of feeble attempts at approaching the open door, but each time she neared the opening, she jumped back and retreated to the farthest corner of the cage. This jumping back is a behavior I've observed many times with wild ravens when they have been given food that is unfamiliar to them. It is a fear response, and we all pitied Wak-Waa and her fear of being free.

Late that afternoon, Chuck took her extra food as he had always done. When he approached her with the food, she performed a submissive posture and cooed at him. This was the first time she'd ever done that. This formerly haughty, courageous raven was seeking any port in the storm for comfort, and on that day she chose Chuck. After several days of nearing the doorway and jumping back, Wak-Waa finally gained the courage to cross the threshold. She was tentative at first, leaving only for a moment or two before returning home.

On about the fourth day, she was out for good, returning only at sunset to her home. As had been his routine for so long, Chuck continued to bring her an evening snack. She would "coo" her thanks and retire for the evening. As is always the case, we needed her enclosure for someone else. She was out and about most of the day, using it only for the evening. We decided to cut the apron strings for good and closed the gate to her former home. She was truly on her own.

Once Wak-Waa realized she no longer had her "sanctuary," she began flying. Although capable, she hadn't flown since we had hacked her out. She also had stopped speaking, thank God. I had visions of her soaring through the skies and teaching neighborhood youngsters their first naughty words. "Mommy, that bird said '_____ _____'—what does that mean?" Just as some people can't chew gum and walk at the same time, maybe ravens can't fly and cuss simultaneously. Wak-Waa sure didn't, much to our relief.

Because They Matter   5

Chuck was concerned as to where she would spend her evenings, as we all were. She spent those first few nights in the honey locust tree above her former home. We could hear her talk herself to sleep and were concerned because she seemed agitated and unhappy.

At this point, she still regarded us humans as something to avoid and certainly had no relationship with other ravens—she was alone. Seeing her like this really bothered Chuck, and he resumed his late-afternoon visits to her as she roosted in the locust tree.

One evening Chuck called me from the house to see Wak-Waa. Having decided that the trees were not her cup of tea, she had begun roosting in the hallway of our office building. She obviously felt more content surrounded by walls instead of freedom. Her roost was a metal shelf unit. On this shelf unit was a long-forgotten blue plastic bowl in which she was sitting when Chuck found her. On subsequent nights, she would greet Chuck while perching on the metal shelf, then hop into the bowl to be "tucked in."

This became—and continues to be—their nightly routine. Chuck did change one thing, however, and that one little change let me and Wak-Waa know just how deep his feelings for her went. He replaced her blue bowl with a large plastic tub. He felt that "she just can't be comfortable in that blue thing." I thought this was a very kind gesture on his part, but Wak-Waa took it for something much more. In her addled little bird brain, this was the ultimate in courtship. Chuck unknowingly had proposed to her, and she had accepted. From that moment on, she spent her waking hours decorating her

Because They Matter

home. For several weeks she was busy carrying specially chosen twigs and sticks and placing them into their nest. If one didn't fit properly, she'd throw it to the floor and gripe. Fortunately, she complained in raven-ese, not human-ese. Although feeling secure for the first time since her release, she still rarely spoke English.

When she did use her foul human language, it was generally a total embarrassment to us all. She saved it for tours of elementary schoolchildren and times when our local Department of Fish and Game officials stopped by to visit. To this day, after many years, she still doesn't like children or people in uniforms.

Although she doesn't curse anymore, we still have to put her away for the school tours. She attacks feet and ankles with a vengeance, and we don't want any of the kids being beaten up by our bird. As for our Fish and Game officers, they're on their own. They all know her, as does anyone who has ever visited us. She's just someone we all must endure—our personal cross to bear.

In the late fall of each year, one of Chuck's main duties is to help Wak-Waa clean house. With her supervision, he removes all of her old nesting material so she can redo her home. Because she is very protective of her and Chuck's nest, we never get to see it except at the fall cleaning. It's always full of surprises. Besides the usual twigs and sticks, we've discovered missing forks and spoons from our kitchen, assorted coins, metal fence ties, stuffed animals, price tags from our merchandise and, once, a string-mop head. She has feathered her nest quite well. She has never laid eggs but has certainly performed all of the other maternal functions. If she is a male, she may be waiting for Chuck to lay. If that's the case, she's got a long wait. We've been married for many years, and I know him well. He has never laid an egg.

Her obvious devotion to Chuck and his toward her is amazing. He is allowed to help her arrange her nest "just so." If I or anyone else dare to touch it, we are beset by massive raven ire. Until Wak-Waa and I came to a mutual understanding, I endured scalp attacks, toe and ankle attacks and, embarrassingly enough, a bruised fanny.

My head was viciously pecked one afternoon when I inadvertently ventured too close to her nest while looking for a gardening tool. I didn't know she was taking a siesta, accidentally touched her nest in my search and was wantonly attacked. Visions of Alfred Hitchcock's *The Birds* danced through my head until my best Tippi Hedren screams alerted Chuck to my dilemma. He rushed in and quickly subdued the bird.

"Excuse me, I have blood coming from my head. Do I need a doctor?" I asked.

"No, you're fine, it's just superficial. Wak-Waa, are you all right?" he queried as he soothed her ruffled feathers.

Wak-Waa adores riding on the old golf cart with Chuck. She likes to stand on the passenger's seat and let the wind blow through her feathers in a most alluring way. I suppose this is her equivalent of being a blonde in a convertible, toodling down the freeway. Now *that* used to attract Chuck; nowadays a raven with him on his golf cart headed for the hay barn is about all his old body can take. One lovely summer afternoon, before Wak-Waa and I came to our "understand-

8   *Because They Matter*

ing," Chuck asked me if I'd like to take a little spin on the golf cart with him and help feed the horses. I was thrilled at the invitation as that is usually Wak-Waa's special time with Chuck. He assured me that she wouldn't mind, so I excitedly hopped aboard. Once I was situated, he gently patted the back of the old cart and summoned the bird.

She gingerly hopped on the rear, took one look at me and immediately donned her "mad hat." When Wak-Waa becomes angry or domineering, all of her head and throat feathers blossom upright, resembling a large hat—this is what I refer to as her "mad hat." I thought I might be in trouble, but Chuck assured me that everything was fine.

I relaxed a bit until we got about halfway to the hay barn. Her mad hat was huge, her black eyes were glistening, and without warning she lit passionately into my rear end. Since this didn't hurt nearly as much as my previous scalp attack, I began laughing, which apparently infuriated the wench. Be-

tween my laughing and her wicked attacks to my backside, I sort of rolled off the moving golf cart and landed on the ground. I dusted myself off, assuming that Chuck would stop for me. Instead, my vision as I chased Chuck, the raven and the golf cart, was of Chuck gently patting the passenger's seat, Wak- Waa stepping onto where I had previously been sitting and Chuck gently smoothing her ruffled feathers as they drove along.

I knew then that I had to make this raven understand that I was a worthy adversary and not some elementary schoolchild or a uniformed person she could dominate. I began to stand up to her and exhibit no fear, even during her temper tantrums. I would brush off her attacks, enter her hallway area boldly when I needed to, and ply her with food. Food is the surest way to a raven's heart. This one loves pasta, I discovered. Food and blatant courage became my weapons.

Within time, she grew to accept me as a peer, and when Chuck is not around, she is my constant companion. Regardless of my relationship with her, she will always love Chuck the best. Wherever he is, so is she, within her bounds. She has rarely ventured beyond our four and a half acres.

Although she flies beautifully, the farthest I have ever seen her fly is about a hundred feet beyond our driveway before turning around and coming home. On that occasion, she was following Chuck in the car as he was headed into town. She was not just tailing his car at that time, she was flying eye to eye with Chuck as he drove. He reported later that he told her to go home, which she did.

Our day begins and ends with this raven who has come to mean so much to us both. At sunrise, when we dare peek out our window to glimpse the day, Wak-Waa's is the first face

Because They Matter

we see. Like a sentinel, she waits on our deck from first light until we emerge from the house. If she sees us, she makes the old familiar raven noises—"kwa, kwa, kwa, kwa"—incessantly, until we close our blinds. It's just her good-morning call, and Chuck would panic if he didn't hear her every morning. I miss the sweet music of the phoebes, finches and red-winged blackbirds, which Wak-Waa's big mouth effectively blocks.

Wak-Waa waits for Chuck, and once he goes outside, they are inseparable. As he walks up the steps leading away from our house to begin his day, she is there walking beside him. She flies beautifully, knows his routine and could just as easily fly to meet him at his first stop. Instead, she walks at his pace, sometimes running to catch up with him if she momentarily becomes distracted by a special rock or a morsel of food she buried the week before and only just then remembered. She is always very busy, and I don't see how she manages to fit Chuck into her schedule, but manage she does.

And so their day begins. They jump on the golf cart together to begin the morning feeding. He says "come on" and pats the seat. She echoes his "come on" and jumps on the seat, ready to roll. "Come on" is her only human vocalization anymore; she uses it only in relation to the golf cart and knows exactly what it means.

Together they feed the horses, goats, llamas and Punky the pig. Chuck hauls the food while Wak-Waa chats with the hoofstock. That's her job, and she takes it very seriously. I am sure she is giving them their orders for the day and, being gentle animals, they all agree with her and comply to the letter. Thank goodness she's there to keep them in tow.

After this ritual, Chuck generally returns to the office to handle phone calls and correspondence. She follows and waits —usually patiently—outside the office for him. If I can't find Chuck, I always look for the raven to tell me where he is, as she is always with him. When he leaves in the car, someone must be designated to "raven duty," as Wak-Waa plants her body firmly in front of our car to prevent Chuck from leaving without her. She is totally prepared to let the car go over her body, rather than let him leave her. He always assures her that he'll be right back, but to Wak-Waa, they are empty words, and one of us must forcibly remove her from the driveway to allow Chuck to leave.

Once when Chuck was leaving, we were not around to prevent her daily attempt at suicide, so in desperation he invited her to ride into town with him for a quick errand. She excitedly jumped into the car, took her position in the passenger's seat and "kwa-kwaaed" and pottied all the way into town and back.

When they returned, Chuck cleaned up her messes without complaining but decided then that Wak-Waa would get no more rides into town. I admit I have often thought about taking her on a little jaunt—a one-way trip—but as clever as she is, she'd probably find her way home and proceed to tell on me. So I merely accept her and all her evil doings.

In April 1994, Chuck was invited to join a veterinary delegation to the People's Republic of China. Although not a veterinarian, Chuck has developed an enormous amount of expertise in dealing with wildlife and was invited to offer assistance to the Chinese to help increase the population of the rare giant panda and several species of endangered, indigenous hoofstock.

He was to be gone for nearly three weeks. I knew I would miss him desperately, as we had not been apart for more than a few days since we began this strange life nine years prior. He knew that I and our staff could handle any emergency that came up during that time. His major concern was what to do with Wak-Waa while he was gone. We decided that for her safety we would put her in a flight enclosure for the duration. We figured this would be one less worry for all of us. By coincidence, the available enclosure was the one in which she had begun her life with us.

On the morning of Chuck's departure, he lured her in, kissed her beak and assured her that he'd be back soon. I secretly smirked, knowing that none of the rest of us would be bedeviled during Chuck's absence. A few minutes after we jailed the bird, Chuck's ride to the airport arrived. Knowing how much I'd miss him, I reached up to kiss him goodbye. The man looked at me like I was a total stranger. I poked him and asked what was wrong.

As if he'd been jarred from a nap, he jumped, apologized to me and said he was thinking about Wak-Waa. I really knew then how deeply he cared for her. I think he gave me a peck on the cheek, and I promised him that I wouldn't let anything happen to her. I didn't, but I certainly had a headful of wicked thoughts. If she had been a human rival, I could have dealt with her and won. She isn't human, but nonetheless she's a rival, and I won't win. She is persistent, totally devoted to him, and in my own different way, I love her, too.

I love ravens, not because they're cute and cuddly but because they are not. They are scrappers, not afraid of being brave; they are intelligent, and they like to have a good time. So many wild animals are much too serious and intent on survival to have a little fun once in a while. Not so with ravens. Since they are scavengers, they can always find something to eat. This gives them the time to party a little or just generally wreak havoc somewhere.

Other than being Chuck's "wife" and disliking other ravens, Wak-Waa is a normal, mischievous raven, just out having a few laughs. We don't know her age. She is a mature adult, and ravens can live forty or so years. My hope is that she's about thirty-nine; my fear is that she's only four or five.

Regardless, it looks like the three of us are in it for the duration. We'll do fine as long as we all understand our positions in this odd relationship. So many people who know Wak-Waa and see her constantly with Chuck refer to her as "Chuck's little black dog." Outwardly I laugh and agree, but inwardly I know that she is much more than that, both in Chuck's eyes and in her own impish, intelligent, home-wrecking mind.

Longshot

I am rarely shocked by anything anymore.

Maggots still bother me, and man's inhumanity to other living beings brings me pretty close to the edge of losing it completely. I got the double whammy with Longshot, and I will never forget the agony, the confusion and the fear in the eyes of that coyote. His eyes were the only thing that gave a clue that he was a coyote and that he was still alive. He had been shot, weeks before, judging from his condition. He had a fractured pelvis, a massive infection and was completely hairless, sunburned, dehydrated and dying of malnutrition. His eyes were filled with the truest sadness I have ever seen. In retrospect, we probably should have helped him leave this world then, but knowing the coyote spirit, we decided to let him decide.

We put an IV catheter in his vein and started him on fluids and antibiotics. Our friend Skip Davis, who admires coyotes as much as we do, volunteered to sit with old Longshot three times a day, thirty to forty-five minutes at a time while he was receiving his slow-drip lactated Ringer's. Skip and Longshot developed a relationship during this time. Soft-spoken, Southern-born Skip spent his shifts talking quietly to Longshot, telling him to hang in there and encouraging him to lap chicken broth on those rare occasions when Longshot would raise his pitiful head.

On the third day, Longshot took a deep sigh and put his head down. It was time for him to be somewhere else. Skip and I cried a little—for him and for all coyotes. We buried Longshot with some wild mustard blossoms and a copy of The Serenity Prayer, a gift from Skip.

Coyotes are dying every day because of some human-related incident, either accidental or intentional. The intentional incidents are unforgivable, done by purely ignorant and inhumane human beings who have no idea who a coyote truly is.

Shooting, trapping and poisoning of the coyote may kill individual animals, but not the coyote itself. They value life, freedom and family as much as, if not more than, we humans and will fight to their last breath to preserve any one of these three values.

The coyote, with his music, his joy for life and his will to survive, could teach us all a wonderful lesson, if we as humans could stop the killing and sit back to listen and learn. Thoughts of old Longshot still pass through my mind, and I often think how fine it would have been if someone who didn't love coyotes had been able to sit with Longshot for those three days. Maybe that someone would have learned about coyote spirit and would have been a better human being because of it.

Rasputin

The turkey vulture is a close cousin to the nearly extinct California condor. They are often called buzzards, which is a misnomer and a much less sophisticated term than vulture. Buzzard is the British term for any large bird of prey, equivalent to raptor, which we Yanks use to describe birds of prey.

On the ground the vulture is much like a slightly nervous, bald, elderly gentleman in a black topcoat. They are not handsome but are terribly polite and endearing in their gracious behavior. In the air, the vulture is by far the most graceful, glorious bird of prey I've seen. Watching vultures soar is much like watching an exquisitely choreographed "air dance."

The first inhabitant of our first flight cage was a vulture. He was with us for several months, initially recovering from a broken wing and, later, learning how to fly again in the flight cage. We named him Rasputin, of course. In many cases, we don't know if birds of prey are males or females, so if we name them, it's based on personality or looks, rather than gender. We assign names to birds that are on medication, etc. It's much easier to say, "Did you give antibiotics to Rasputin?" than to say, "Did you medicate the vulture in room one, cage two with the wing-wrap on his left wing?"

Rasputin was a quiet, timid, non-aggressive patient, as most vultures are. Oh, they have their faults as we all do, such as vomiting when threatened and having a very peculiar rank odor about them.

Vultures are garbage collectors, and 99.9 percent of their

diet consists of dead things, either freshly killed or not so freshly killed. Their digestive system is equipped to handle even the most odoriferous of the not so recently departed. Thus when they regurgitate in times of stress, it will clear a room. We are *very* careful not to stress our vulture clientele. Their rank odor is caused in part by the fact that they pass their urates down their legs to keep them cool. In other words, they go to the bathroom on themselves.

Their bald red head, which often takes people aback, serves a great purpose. With what they eat and the manner in which they eat it, a headful of feathers would quickly rot and fall off. Mother Nature surely averted a faux pas when the vulture turned out bald! Strategically placed on this unique red head are two of the most beautiful eyes imaginable.

I am a great eye watcher (windows of the soul, you know). In the coyotes' eyes I see courage; in the ravens' eyes, intelligence, and in the vultures' eyes there is kindness and innocence. Perhaps others would see different things, but I have gazed into thousands of eyes, and these are my perceptions.

There was nothing remarkable about Rasputin's several months with us, at least not to us. His wing healed beautifully, he was able to soar in the flight cage and rebuild his atrophied pectoral muscles and eventually regain his freedom. Rehabbing and releasing is commonplace to us, yet to Rasputin, it was his life. He had been given a whole new life because we were able to help.

What was remarkable to us and continues to be is that not until we released Rasputin did we begin to have the influx of vulture visitors that we now have.

Because They Matter

Earlier I mentioned that a vulture's diet consists of 99.9 percent "dead things." Some would say 100 percent; however, on several occasions I have seen vultures, especially juveniles, eating dry dog food, popcorn and blades of grass. We do not deal with a large volume of injured or orphaned vultures at our wildlife facility for two reasons: Vultures ground-nest, so babies don't fall out of fifty-foot palm trees; vultures eat carrion, therefore they don't get injured while hunting for live prey.

The injured ones we take in have usually been hit by cars; these slow-moving birds are often seen eating road kills in the middle of busy roads and just don't have the takeoff power that smaller birds have. The other injured ones are those with gunshot wounds. Although federally protected, these lovely creatures are routinely blasted out of the sky by ignorant yahoos with guns.

A very tragic and painful one-third of the cases that come to us are those vultures that have been poisoned. These rarely survive. Often, people put out various poisons to rid themselves of troublesome squirrels, rats and other rodents. Many of these poisons are transferred up the food chain. In many cases, if a vulture (or other animal) eats a poisoned animal, the poison is then transferred to that animal. Secondary poisoning is slower and very agonizing for the victim. On a lighter note, most of the vultures we see are just neighborhood residents who stop by to visit, hang out and once in a while have a morsel or two. These we enjoy the most—vultures just being vultures. No one is ill or injured. No one needs our help. Someone, somewhere, just told them that this is a great place to visit. Every afternoon we watch ten or twelve vultures on our property, either eating, soaring above our heads, roosting or perching with their wings spread. Late summer is the best time, as many juveniles stop by with their parents to socialize.

The juveniles are indistinguishable from their parents, size-wise. Up close, however, it's easy to spot a youngster. The young vulture's head is either dark gray or black, and the younger of the juveniles have little white wispy hair-like feathers covering their heads. They are really cute! They are also very clumsy, not having developed the grace that comes with age. We've watched juveniles attempt to land on telephone wires, obviously for the first time. They are like disabled aircraft attempting to land and often go – – – over teakettle during their tries. Somehow they manage to recoup their dignity and eventually conquer their ineptness.

Many vultures roost in our tall trees for the night, and apparently because they enjoy each other's company they often roost together and all too often on thin branches not strong enough to hold one, let alone six. On into the evening, the night is filled with the sound of branches snapping, wings flapping and groggy vultures attempting to resettle for the night. I've often wondered what a stranger might visualize upon hearing the snapping, flapping and occasional hissing that is so familiar to us.

Because They Matter

Vultures rarely get riled, but when they do they hiss. You know you've made an enemy when you've got a hissing, vomiting vulture on your exam table! The only time I've ever seen a vulture hiss in the wild was when one was politely roosting on one of our tall power poles and a pesky raven decided he wanted that particular roost. The raven sneaked up behind and pulled the vulture's tail feathers. The vulture hissed, attempted to re-roost and was beset by the raven again. The vulture lost that skirmish and relocated himself away from the impish raven.

As I've said, they are very polite. From a distance I have often watched several vultures watching a red-tailed hawk eat to its heart's content. Only when the red-tail is finished and flies away do the vultures even think about moving in for their lunch. While I'm sure they'd much enjoy the choice parts rather than the leftovers, still they patiently sit and wait their turn.

If you are fortunate enough to observe a kettle of vultures dancing in the sky, doff your hat to these genteel "sanitation engineers" and enjoy the ballet!

Terry

Springtime is an extremely difficult time for all of us involved in wildlife rehabilitation. Our workload is the heaviest, as we're dealing not only with the usual injured wildlife but also with the orphaned babies of all species. There are many days, referred to as "death days," when our losses are so heavy, despite all our efforts, that many of us wish we had chosen a different path to follow.

There are also those days that bring us such joy that we can't imagine doing anything else! The good days are those in which we finally observe a young pigeon eating on its own for the first time, or when we finally remove a pin from the badly broken wing of a barn owl and watch her take her first flight after three months of hospitalization.

Even better days are those in which a baby corvid (crows, ravens and jays) enters our center. We are always distressed at accepting any orphaned baby and know it would be so much better off with its "bird mommy," but it often just does not happen that way.

Baby crows are the most delightful, and when an orphaned one enters our hospital, we know we're going to have a good time. Nowadays we never raise a corvid alone. We network with our sister organizations all over California to ensure that virtually no animal that comes to our center as an orphan is raised without same or similar species companionship. In our early years, we accepted and raised those who came to us without the networking abilities we now have.

Terry was our first and only baby crow that spring so many years ago. The name Terry was a shortened version of pterodactyl, which is what this little nude, moist, warm creature resembled when he came to us. At that time, our hospital was makeshift, with all species together in the same room and hospital cages stacked one on top of the other. Terry's cage was on the floor to facilitate feeding him and also to prevent accidents such as his falling onto the floor as he became an active fledgling.

Crows are extremely intelligent, and after several weeks Terry began to associate feet with food. From his unlofty perch on the ground, he began to realize that the sight of feet usually meant that he was going to eat. Terry loved to eat, consequently he grew to love people's feet.

Terry's foot fetish stayed with him until adulthood, at which time more important things like sex began to enter his mind. Having been raised with no other crows, Terry bonded with humans. I can still see him in my mind's eye as a young teenager, having just been released, following any one of us around, staring at our shoes and gaping to be fed the entire time—gaping at our shoes, mind you, as if they had some magical way to provide food! In his crow brain, Terry remembered that shoes brought food before and couldn't seem to understand why they couldn't do it now.

Terry stayed with us for about a year and probably caused us more worry than any other animal we've had. For the first nine months of his life, Terry was *always* with us.

Being sociable birds, crows tend to congregate together. Poor little confused Terry, having no other crows around, mistakenly thought he was supposed to socialize with us. Break times during that period consisted of five or six adults sitting in the shade sipping coffee and enjoying the peace and quiet of the Ramona countryside, and one little black crow walking from one set of feet to another, cawing, gaping, begging the shoes for food. When that didn't get the shoes' attention, he would untie the shoelaces or peck at the soles.

If that *still* didn't get food, he moved up to the socks (with human ankles inside) and pecked. This usually caused a piece of doughnut or a potato chip to appear. If that didn't work, he went straight to the top. The little fool would jump onto the head of a shoe wearer and peck just once as if to say, "Excuse me, is anyone home down there? I really need my snack."

Terry was a pest, an imp, and nearly drove us crazy with his antics. He constantly bedeviled Archie, our since-departed elderly orange cat who helped us run the place. Archie's tail was more than Terry could handle. He really wanted one of his own and kept trying to steal Archie's. Dear, sweet Archie took all this mischief in stride and would only raise his head and glare on those frequent occasions when his slumber was interrupted by the evil one pulling his tail.

Terry kept us either laughing or cursing his entire stay with us. If he wanted something, he just stole it. Everything belonged to him. He would even go so far as to unzip my purse, rifle through it to find what he wanted and gleefully fly away.

More than once, I found items from my purse that Terry had left on the roof, dumped in water tubs or buried in flower pots. He just couldn't help himself. He was great at burying things, especially snacks that he wanted to save for later. We'd all watch when he would meticulously bury a prize doughnut morsel, step back to make sure it was completely covered from all angles, then cover it with more leaves and twigs just to make sure. Amazingly enough, he would invariably return to the burial spot, hours or even days later, and retrieve the delicacy.

One day, I did get back at him. Several of us were enjoying ice cream bon bons one hot summer day when you-know-who came out of nowhere to harass our feet. Just to get some peace and to shut him up, I gave Terry a whole bon bon. This was so exciting for him and such a coveted prize, that after tasting a bit of it, he just had to bury it.

After about thirty minutes, he decided to have another bite. Much to his surprise (and he truly had an amazed look on his face), he uncovered a gooey, melted, warm mess that even a crow couldn't eat. He was mad and I was elated. That's the only time I ever was able to fool the little fool.

Because They Matter

As pesky as he was, we panicked when he wasn't around. Too many people in our area don't love the crows as we do, and we were concerned for his safety when he wasn't close by. Up until he was nine or ten months old, he didn't leave the property. After that point, he began to make road trips, which frightened us to no end.

The amazing thing about his excursions is that he visited people who knew him. His first venture from us lasted several hours. He had not been around for a while when a close friend called in to report that Terry had been following his kids around all morning, cawing at their feet and eating saltine crackers. Shortly thereafter, Terry returned home, much to our relief. We wanted him to leave us and be free, but not while he was still so people-friendly.

As I look back, that day was Terry's turning point. He began to stay away more often, always returning home late in the afternoon. His longest road trip lasted two days. We had no idea where he had been and didn't appreciate his cavalier attitude upon returning. He didn't care that we had been worried sick. Later, we found out that he had spent that lost weekend with friends Bea and Billy Hoskins, who live a mile or so from us.

Bea and Billy had houseguests for the weekend, two invited guests, and one not. Early Saturday morning the four humans were enjoying fruit cups and coffee on the balcony. Out of nowhere, a crow appeared, helped himself to his favorite fruits and a sip or two of coffee. Bea, Billy and guests just laughed and enjoyed the uninvited guest. The same routine happened the next morning as well. Later that day, Bea called us to see if Terry had run away from home. We told her that he had, and when she related the fruit cup story, we knew where Terry had been. He returned home later and acted as if he'd never left.

At this time, in addition to making road trips, Terry began developing relationships with other wild crows who call our place "home base." His time was spent traveling and chatting with other crows, leaving very little time to hang around with us. At about a year old, Terry no longer acknowledged our existence and became a real crow. Although it's been years, I'm sure he's still part of the group that lives here and delights us with their antics.

I believe Terry is still with us because I choose to believe that. In releasing our animals, we can never be sure that they really fare well in the real world. We can only prepare them to the best of our limited abilities. There are things, however, that we can't protect them from, and people like Harry (not his real name) are at the top of that list.

Harry is a benign-looking Ramona resident whose ignorant attitudes have the potential for destroying much of our native wildlife for generations to come. My encounter with him started innocently enough, as he is a Boy Scout leader who had arranged for his troop of a dozen boys to visit our wildlife hospital and rehabilitation center. We generally enjoy groups of kids touring our facility because they are our future, and if we can impart some of our knowledge regarding the importance of all our native wild species, perhaps the children will leave with a little more respect and compassion for other beings.

Because They Matter

I greeted the kids and Harry and explained in a nutshell what kind of work we do here. The first words out of Harry's mouth were "Are you one of those environmental nuts?" I kind of felt a sinking feeling in my stomach at that point and began to feel that I had lost the whole group before I even started. I told Harry that I was very concerned about our environment and hoped that he was, too. Harry smirked and I looked at the faces of those boys and, depressingly enough, saw twelve little Harrys standing before me.

The first enclosure I took Harry and his little clones to housed eight juvenile crows, babies from that spring who were learning how to be crows prior to being released. As I explained this to the boys, Harry asked me if I wanted about fifty more crows. I asked him what he meant, and he explained that he had some pesky crows on his property that he was going to have to shoot. He said this with a smile on his face, and I became enraged.

I told him that even if he was joking, that was a nasty thing to say to someone who cares deeply about all wildlife. I also told him that he was setting a terrible example for those boys. Harry gave me a condescending smile and a pat on the shoulder. I really wanted to slug him at that point, but I stuck my hands in my pockets and continued the tour.

It was a quick tour, and I'm sure the boys learned nothing from me that day. Harry had already influenced them, and there was no way that I, in just half an hour, could reverse the damage he'd done. As the boys were leaving, we stopped at one of our large rehabilitative flight cages, housing our eagles, hawks, vultures and owls. One by one, as if on cue, these twelve little boys pointed their index fingers, aimed and pretended to shoot these birds. I quietly ended the tour, came into the house and cried for those damaged little boys, for the crows, the birds of prey and for Harry and the beauty he will never see.

Old 2.5

Old 2.5 came to us early in our rehab work.

Our office was the makeshift hospital, and makeshift it was. Cage units with injured birds lined one wall, the floor housed cages of orphaned or discarded domestic kittens. A desk and a sliding glass door leading outside occupied the opposite wall. Visitors and staff were constantly in and out—a totally inadequate situation for the wildlife.

Chuck responded to a coyote call in our neighborhood early one morning. Apparently a coyote had been chased by dogs, cornered up against a fence and had been unable to escape. According to the reporting party, the coyote looked to be in pretty bad shape, possibly injured by the dogs.

Chuck managed to contain him and bring him to our center. He was dehydrated but not bleeding anywhere and had no apparent *new* injuries. He also did not have most of his left rear leg, most probably the result of being caught in a steel-jaw trap and chewing off his own leg to escape. His right front leg was severely deformed. The paw was completely turned inward and had been for so long that an enormous hard callous had formed on what we would refer to as the top of our hand at the wrist joint. He walked on this part to compensate for the missing rear limb.

Again, these were old injuries, and he had obviously been surviving just fine without our help. That fact didn't dawn on us until later, however.

The dehydration, as a result of a tremendous adrenaline

rush from being chased and cornered by the dogs, had us concerned. We valiantly placed an IV catheter in his good foreleg and gave him 200 ccs of lactated Ringer's solution. We put him in a wire cage covered with a sheet to minimize the stress of gawkers in and out of the office/hospital.

God, we were so ignorant in those days! We gave him a big bowl of water, some food and kept an eye on him all that day. He, apparently, was keeping an eye on us also. He watched us come and go through the sliding glass door. He never flinched or acted unduly upset, he just sat quietly and watched us as we watched him.

Around eight that evening, we made sure that the glass door to the office was closed when we finished all our chores. Old 2.5 hadn't moved a muscle, not even for a sip of water. We left the office and retired for the night. We talked that evening about 2.5's situation, since we were new to coyotes and weren't sure if he'd live through the night. If he lived and recovered, what would we do? Could we, in good conscience, release this disabled coyote? This was quite a quandary for new rehabbers.

Chuck and I were outside by seven the next morning to check on our new patient. As we approached the office, we saw that the sliding door was open about six inches. We were certain we had closed it the night before.

We quietly entered the office to check on old 2.5. Half the office was in a shambles, with blood everywhere; the desk had been toppled and gnawed, and 2.5's cage was demolished and empty. No other cages in the room had been disturbed. The room was full of kittens and other animals, yet the only

Because They Matter

part of the room 2.5 was interested in was the part that led to the outside.

During the cleanup, we retraced his steps: He quietly ate all of his food, drank his bowl of water and removed his IV catheter. He then chewed his way out of the wire cage, causing its demise, and lost a tooth in the process. This accounted for the blood everywhere. He gnawed our desk, opened its drawers and toppled it, just for effect. Then he nudged open the glass door and quietly left our wonderful accommodations.

He had been watching us all day just to find out where the exit was! He was very smart. A disabled coyote learns to rely on smarts rather than physical ability.

As I mentioned earlier, the office was smeared with blood from his lost tooth, yet there wasn't a drop of blood outside the office door, thus making him impossible to track. His "auto-release" solved a dilemma for us and gave us a much better insight into the survival instinct of the coyote in general and old 2.5 in particular.

We and our volunteers conducted an all-out property search for him. We searched our nearly five acres and the four acres across the street, which are renowned coyote hunting fields. We found no trace of our "Houdini." However, with the cunning abilities of the coyote, we could have been six inches away from old 2.5 and never have seen him.

We are confident that he's still out there and doing fine. On part of our property is a dense growth of honeysuckle, where wild bunnies and small birds cavort. Chuck swears that the hair on the back of his neck rises when he's out there at sunset. He's sure that somewhere in that honeysuckle, a pair of golden, wily-and-wiser-than-we-are eyes are watching him.

Señora Possum

This charming lady possum was found on the roadside near the U.S.-Mexico border. She had been grazed by a car and was quite stunned and shocky when she arrived at our center, courtesy of a kind businessman who took the time to help an animal in need. She was semiconscious with seven youngsters clinging tenaciously to her when she arrived early one March morning.

Had this sweet possum known what was in store for her at our center, she may have—had she been given a choice—opted to stay on the side of the road!

We checked her out and found her injuries to be minor. We treated her for shock and administered some subcutaneous fluids just to boost her spirits. Her babies looked healthy and were at the age where they were still nursing once in a while but also eating solid food. We carefully placed the frazzled little mother and her pretty babies in a large carrier and provided them with plenty of food and water.

By the next day, Señora and her babies looked fine and all the food had disappeared. We figured that in a few days, we'd shake this family loose to let them begin a new life.

In the meantime, however, we took in two little Mickey Mouse–looking possums who were about the same age as Señora's babies. They were doing okay under our care but really could have used some possum-mama companionship. Michelle and I kept ogling Señora and her babies, so healthy and well cared for, and decided that since possums have thirteen nipples and since these babies were semi-weaned just as Señora's were, maybe she could handle two more.

Señora graciously accepted these two extra babies as her own. Female possums make excellent surrogate mothers so, unfortunately for Señora, her stay with us turned out to be longer than any of us anticipated. She really couldn't complain at this point, since she was staying in the best possum hotel in town, was being served the most nutritious and delicious food possible, and all she had to do was offer a mother's comfort to nine little possums.

A week or so went by, and Señora's youngsters were no longer nursing, just cuddling with her. Lo and behold—we took in six more babies, a bit younger than Señora's. We didn't have the heart to overload her, so we tube-fed the babies (possums have no suckling reflex, so a bottle doesn't work). Although tubing is risky, it's necessary until we can get them to lap their formula.

The six new ones were doing well, and we knew they'd soon be lapping formula and visiting the Gerber's garden. We use a lot of human baby food in our weaning process and have found Gerber's strained plums to be a real hit. These six babies were in a plastic cat carrier on a heating pad in the medical center; they couldn't have been cozier, or so we thought.

Staff members generally arrive at daylight during "baby season" to begin feeding all the babies, as we feed for twelve to fourteen hours straight on a daily basis. Michelle arrived first, and when I got to the medical center about forty-five minutes later, she informed me that we had lost two of our young possums.

"How could they have died?" I asked her, as they had been fine the night before.

"They didn't die," she replied, "they are really *lost*—somewhere in this room."

When Michelle first entered the medical center that morning, she found four of the six babies curled up asleep on the floor of the main room. She had been unable to locate the other two. Somehow they all had gotten out of their carrier. We did a thorough search and found nothing. We knew they hadn't been abducted by alien possum snatchers and that we'd eventually find these two travelers. We also knew that we had about a hundred baby mouths screaming for breakfast and clean carriers, so Michelle and I got busy with our morning routine.

Señora and her nine babies had really made a mess the night before (one of those wild possum parties you often read about), so they all needed to be transferred to a new home. This transfer involved donning my mammal gloves (heavy-duty gloves reinforced with steel staples that will lessen an injury if a wild animal bites) and moving Señora and her nine bambinos, one at a time, into their clean cage.

As I moved them, I counted heads and examined each baby to make sure that each one was okay. To my surprise, Señora had eleven babies. Two looked strangely familiar and were a bit younger than the others. I let Michelle know that I had found our two travelers—all cozy, warm and content against Señora's belly.

If possums could talk, Señora would have been screaming at us, or begging for mercy by this time. Our two little renegades had little possum grins on their faces and looked so happy, so without hesitation Michelle and I slipped in the other four right next to their siblings. If a possum glare could kill, Michelle and I would have been unable to finish our morning chores due to our untimely demise. Señora, however, never showed any reluctance toward these orphans and cuddled with each and every one as if she had given birth to all fifteen.

Señora's true test came one rainy April morning when our friend, volunteer and topnotch animal rescuer Barbara Woodhill drove up our driveway with an ice-cold, barely alive "pouch baby."

Apparently, a youngster had found this baby after the family dog had killed the mother possum. The boy took this prize to school for "show and tell." When the school secretary called Barbara to report the incident, Barbara quickly drove to the school, located the right classroom and found thirty kids and a teacher gaping at this half-dead baby possum. Obviously unaware of the fact that this little possum was just about dead and that exhibiting any wild animal for "show and tell" is a very cruel thing to do, the teacher (after a quick bit of education) gladly let Barbara take the baby.

Thorough person that Barbara is, and always ready to go that extra mile for an animal in need, she called the mother of the youngster to tell her about the possum and our center, and asked her to search the area for other babies.

As luck would have it, the mother found two more limp but living babies in her yard and was more than willing to bring them to our center.

These three babies were in bad shape; one we were unable to save. The only chance for the other two was Señora's motherly touch (and pouch). Her pouch was empty but she was lactating, so we quickly positioned the two remaining babies inside Señora's pouch and hoped for the best. Well, Señora did her best. The youngsters thrived, and within a few weeks these two healthy Mickey Mouse look-alikes began hanging onto Señora's back along with the other fifteen juvenile possums.

As spring approached summer, Señora and all her kids were still with us, and the number of kids had grown by about a dozen more. During that baby season, when we took in an

orphaned possum and verified that it was otherwise healthy but just too young to be on its own, we placed it in the Possum Hotel, owned and operated by Señora Possum.

Until their release late that summer, Señora and her nearly thirty children were usually curled up together, dozing peacefully in their dark, cozy shelter, with Señora on the bottom, only her head exposed, and a horde of Mickey Mouses covering the rest of her body.

Once in a while, however, we'd find Señora away from the kids, on the highest ledge in the "hotel," asleep—all by herself. Like all mothers, she needed a break from the kids, I guess.

The only thing I couldn't understand was why this normally docile, excellent mother possum would bare her teeth, drool and growl every time Michelle or I would approach her enclosure. On second thought, if I were a mother possum already exhausted from caring for my own kids, and two weird-looking other creatures kept bringing me other possums' babies to care for, I'd probably do more than just bare my teeth, drool and growl.

Bad Bob

Bad Bob came to us on December 29, 1990.

I vividly remember that day because while Chuck had gone to Palm Springs to rescue this bobcat, I received the tragic news that a beloved staff member, Steve Stemper, had passed away due to a massive heart attack. Steve was only thirty-two years old, so this was a tremendous blow to all of us. All the while during our crying and grieving for Steve, we were endeavoring to bring this bobcat back from near death.

Attempting to pull this cat back and truly just wanting to cry for Steve made that day one of my worst ever. Steve, my friend, was gone. The bobcat's chances were basically nil, and I desperately wanted to be somewhere else.

Long-time volunteers Stan and Cheryll Brown, Jill Estensen and Chuck and I inserted an IV catheter with a slow drip of lactated Ringer's and began the physical exam of our comatose bobcat. He weighed eighteen pounds, was severely malnourished and dehydrated and had a major eyesight problem (resembling cataracts). He appeared to be either elderly or at least middle-aged, judging by his overall condition.

Eighteen pounds and starving to death was difficult for us to believe, as we deal with many injured adult bobcats and have found that their weights range from nine to fourteen pounds—well fed. This was a *big* old cat!

To our surprise, he lived through that first night and was semiconscious the next morning. We actually had to physically restrain him (chemical restraint was out of the question in his weakened condition) to administer his regimen of IV fluids that day. When we reached the day when one of us was in danger of losing a valued body part in order to administer the IV fluids to "Bad Bob" (hence the name), we decided to offer him a liquid gruel consisting of chicken broth and puréed meat instead. Even in his still weakened condition, he readily lapped his food.

Within a week he was eating solid food and gaining weight. It should be noted that we could only tell by observation that Bob was gaining weight—there was no way that any of us could get him to stand on our bathroom scales! Bob grew stronger every day. His appetite was enormous. Our goal at this point was to make him strong enough to withstand anesthesia, since we still had the eyesight problem to deal with.

After about a month, Bob was as healthy as he could be. Chuck prepared a low dosage of a mild sedative and, using the eight-foot pole syringe, zapped Bad Bob in his butt. Bob was not grateful to us for saving his life, so we took great care to avoid his wrath. Chuck was able to use his pole syringe from outside of Bob's enclosure. We entered the enclosure only after Bob had become quite groggy. We quickly crated him up and took him to Dr. Don Wood, our veterinarian.

In addition to the eye exam, Dr. Wood did a blood panel, a feline leukemia test and weighed Bob. In his month with us, Bob had gained seven pounds. He now weighed twenty-five pounds but still looked thin. His blood work was all within normal range for an elderly cat, and he was negative for feline leukemia. This was all good news, but his eyesight problem was another story.

Because They Matter

Old age compounded with his malnutrition had really diminished his vision. The old age made it difficult for him to hunt adequately, causing the malnourishment, which further diminished his vision, which made it even more difficult for Bob to hunt. Bad Bob had been caught in what we would call a vicious circle. This circle, as cruel as it may seem to us, is in fact the law of nature. We as humans had interfered with this natural cycle, and the decision of life or death for him was now in our hands. Bad Bob's eyesight would not improve, consequently there was no hope of releasing this magnificent creature back into the wild.

We made perhaps a very selfish decision that day. We decided not to euthanize Bad Bob but to keep him as a permanent resident. He had shown such exuberance over being fed on a regular basis and seemed to us to be relatively content in his small enclosure. Also, I think we were tired of Death. We had had to euthanize several terribly injured animals that week and were still trying to bounce back from Steve's death as well.

Assuming that cranky old Bad Bob would be with us a while, we constructed a 2,000-cubic-foot chain-link enclosure for him on a secluded part of the property. He had logs, grass and a comfortable shelter in which to sleep. Bad Bob slept a lot, as many senior citizens do. However, he was always wide awake at feeding times.

He became so routinized in his nearly three years with us that if we dared to pass his enclosure at what he knew was either snack time or dinner time without stopping to feed him, he would stand at his entry gate growling and snarling at us. He was so beautiful yet so frightening.

Because he was "special," and because we dared not enter his enclosure to clean it without first presenting food to Bob, he got two meals a day instead of the usual one evening feeding we give to other recuperating bobcats. Bad Bob ate and continued to grow. He was, by far, the largest bobcat I've ever seen. After six months with us, he was a trim thirty-six pounds! Bob maintained this weight for most of his time with us. Except for his old foggy eyes, he was a truly exquisite cat.

We continued to debate over his fate. He looked so healthy. We had all seen him ogling ground squirrels playing outside his enclosure and had found remains of hapless squirrels who had meandered through the chain link of his home. The old boy could still hunt and wish. It was the wishing part that really bothered me.

During the spring when the squirrels were abundant, Bad Bob would spend hours watching them at play through his old man's eyes. I would watch him watch them and fight back this tremendous urge to fling his gate open and let him try for "just one." He was an old hunter, one who hunted just to stay alive. Old habits die hard, and it was hard to watch him covet his past life. Only good sense restrained me from releasing Bad Bob. His eyes were foggier every month, and he would not have survived for more thane two weks in the wild.

Many humans like to live lives in which they can feel some sense of fulfillment, so that as they are dying, their last thoughts are that they are leaving this world a far better place than it would have been without them. I would like to leave this world in that way, yet I doubt that Bad Bob had these same thoughts. Whether he felt that way or not, Bob left us

Because They Matter

with a living legacy. Besides the kittens he may have sired during his many years as a handsome, virile young bobcat, Bob gave new life to three desperately ill bobcat kittens during his time with us.

Bad Bob was ours for three springtimes. In our work, spring is called baby season, the time of the year when orphaned wildlife of all species come to us, including baby bobcats. Sometimes baby mammals come to us as true orphans (the mother dies), or they come to us because they are ill or injured. Wild-animal mothers do the best they can in caring for their babies, yet they must also be selective. If a wild baby is born deformed or becomes ill or injured, the baby is discarded because mother knows that she cannot adequately care for problems like this and must focus her attention on the well and strong. Again, such is the law of nature. It is neither cruel nor kind—it just *is*.

During those three baby seasons, we took in three abandoned baby bobcats, severely anemic, dehydrated and hungry. These babies were past weaning age but young enough to still be with their moms. In each of these cases, because he was our healthiest bobcat, Bad Bob (unwillingly) donated his blood for whole-blood transfusions to these sick babies. In all three cases, the babies survived and were later released back into the wild.

Having Bad Bob donate his blood was no easy task for us or him. Needless to say, for our own safety we had to sedate him using our eight-foot pole syringe. Sedating any wild animal is a very risky procedure because not all wild animals react to chemical restraint in the way one would expect. Many animals, especially the predators, fight the effects of anesthesia tooth and nail. In most cases, the anesthesia wins, but not easily.

In 1991 and 1992, old Bob donated fifteen ccs of whole blood each time and came out of the anesthesia beautifully. In the spring of 1993, Bob went down smoothly and donated his blood. Coming up this time, however, was very difficult for him. It was several days before the "groggy look" disappeared from his face. His appetite remained undiminished, fortunately, but Chuck decided that he could no longer subject this majestic old cat to the rigors of anesthesia.

Bad Bob spent the rest of the spring and summer of 1993 undisturbed and apparently as content as any captive wild animal can be. By early fall, his appetite decreased, he lost some weight and began drinking water, which I had never before seen him do. He continued his morning and evening routines of waiting for his food, yet often didn't eat it when we fed him. We didn't want to anesthetize him again for a checkup, fearing he wouldn't come out of it, so we decided to closely monitor him, watching his appetite and other behaviors. Some days he ate, others he didn't. His feces appeared normal, but there seemed to be an abundance of urine.

After several days of not eating and considerable weight loss, we decided to sedate Bob, knowing the risks involved yet not wanting him to suffer from some terrible yet treatable disease. Dr. Wood took urine and blood samples, which revealed adult-onset diabetes. If Bad Bob had been a domestic animal, daily insulin shots may have helped; being a wild animal, daily injections would have been extremely stressful,

Because They Matter

dangerous and possibly counterproductive. We made the decision in November 1993 to euthanize this dear, lovely old bobcat before life became too painful for him.

Sometimes we humans, and in particular those of us who often deal with mortally ill or injured "other beings," often feel the need to justify our actions if for no one other than ourselves. Painlessly euthanizing an animal is easy; living with it later is not. We needed to reaffirm our belief that we had done the right thing for Bad Bob. Chuck and Dr. Wood performed a ne-cropsy (an autopsy on an animal), which revealed a completely nonfunctioning pancreas (the insulin-producing organ). Euthanasia was the most humane thing we could have done for him.

The comfort we take from this experience is knowing that, somewhere out there, three bobcats are running wild and free, with the blood of the grandest bobcat I've ever known coursing through their veins.

"Can-Do" Michelle

People who choose to work with animals are an unusual breed of folks. Those of us who do so all have our different reasons for being involved in generally low-paying careers and very often in dirty, frightening and dangerous situations. Michelle Lyons' reasons for working with us for so many years are simple: She loves animals of any kind, and she loves to feed animals who like to eat, as most wild animals do. I have often said that if Michelle were put in charge of a "Feed the World" program, no one would ever go hungry.

Michelle's urge to fill the stomachs and crops of the native wildlife under our care and her love of botany, in particular, native plants, have made her an ace dietitian at our facility. Not only do our scavengers and herbivores sleep with full tummies, they sleep with tummies full of their natural diets—those seeds, fruits, berries and plants that occur naturally in their environment. These are the things they must learn to eat, and Michelle searches our Southern California wilderness areas for tidbits to feed our clients. Once in a while she goes a little overboard, and we've had to yank her out of precarious situations. When she's hunting for native plants for use as food or habitat construction, she forgets herself and becomes the absent-minded professor.

Michelle's a great teacher and was explaining to me, one day, the benefits of a patch of doveweed we were examining. As she was describing its usefulness to our wildlife, I was keeping one eye and one ear on her spiel and the other eye and ear on oncoming traffic, to which Michelle had become oblivious. This particular patch of doveweed was growing up through the asphalt of a very busy main thoroughfare.

When I saw the semi headed our way, I grabbed her elbow and ushered her to the shoulder of the road. She didn't miss a beat and continued extolling the praises of that stupid doveweed. This is the Michelle our newer staff members know and respect. Only a few of us know the other Michelle, and it is this Michelle who typifies what it takes to be a "real" wildlife rehabilitator.

At her tallest, she's around five-feet-two. She's Basque, which is either a plus or a minus—I haven't yet figured out which. When I first met her, I liked her very much but had my doubts about her abilities. She was so cute and so short! On her first day as a volunteer, she proved herself twice, and I have never since had any apprehensions. As a matter of fact, the courage she has shown has put all of us to shame.

Chuck's criterion for new volunteers used to be based on how well they could rake a pasture. No wimps were allowed. On her first day, Michelle gained Chuck's ultimate respect by raking like a wild woman, so he was duly impressed. Later that same day, we retrieved a bobcat, obviously on her last legs, from an area close to Ramona. This was to be Michelle's first experience with a wild animal.

This cat was a definite goner, going through violent "death throes" by the time she arrived here. The odd thing was that although this cat was extremely dehydrated, there were no obvious injuries or signs of illness. Chuck decided, despite the cat's violent "last breath" behavior, to try to insert an IV

Because They Matter

catheter and give her some lactated Ringer's solution. To calm the cat's seizures, he first administered a mild sedative to allow us to help her. The cat calmed down, Chuck got the catheter in and began a slow drip.

All this time, Michelle and I were sitting mesmerized by the beauty of this cat and by the tragedy of knowing that she would probably die. Once the cat was sedated and her veins were being pumped full of sustenance, Michelle began crying softly, and she and I started pulling ticks from the cat's emaciated body. We kept the catheter in her vein and set up the cat for the night, doubtful that she would be alive in the morning, but hoping anyway.

She was still with us the next morning, no longer seizuring, a little stronger but still manageable. We filled her with more lactated Ringer's and left a dish of chicken broth for her, just in case. By that afternoon, she had consumed the chicken broth and was standing up. Michelle cried again. This was her first bobcat, and she had been witness to the miracles that sometimes happen here.

We had blood work done on the cat, which revealed nothing major wrong with her other than malnutrition. Another case of loss of habitat. By the third day, the cat was more than just standing, she was eating and drinking enormous volumes and, for the first time, eliminating enormous volumes.

Michelle and I had to clean her room. Only one of us should have been in there with her, but I wanted Michelle to experience the raw fear that comes from being in close quarters with a wild animal. I was scared to death but knew it had to be done. Michelle was also scared to death and spent most of the time hiding behind me and saying those deleted expletives you often read about. She didn't give up, though, and helped me clean the room.

It was a horrifying experience, and a less-brave person would have left and not returned. Michelle stayed with me that day, and after many years of equally harrowing experiences, she is still here. I have never once doubted her courage or her commitment. The bobcat quickly regained her strength, her weight and, several weeks later, her freedom. Michelle went on the release and cried—again.

Not long after volunteer Michelle became staff member Michelle, we received a call on an injured fawn. These are the most heartbreaking. The deer are so delicate and so frightened that often those with just minor injuries succumb to the stress involved with their rescue. Younger fawns handle rescue and treatment a little better than juveniles, so we fervently hoped that this was a young one we were going for. Chuck gathered all our available staff and volunteers and the necessary gear and headed out.

The fawn turned out to be a teenager, hit by a car, dangling a rear leg but still mobile. This was a tough one. Michelle, Chuck and six or seven others spent hours chasing this youngster throughout the entire eighteen holes of a local golf course. At one point the staff formed a blockade with Michelle in hot pursuit of the fawn. She knew she had him, and in her usual emotional way she began sobbing as she tackled this frightened, badly injured deer. His injuries were terrible, which compounded Michelle's agony. The leg had two compound fractures. There was no chance of repair so the little guy was euthanized. Michelle did not weep at this, as she had helped bring a peaceful end to an enormous amount of suffering.

If not for her moxie and persistence, the fawn would have been in agony for probably several days before dying from his injuries. Introducing a new staff member or volunteer to Death is not often easy on us or them. Michelle had the ability to realize that her energy was not wasted on rescuing this fawn only to euthanize him later. She had helped him and was pleased that she had done so.

One fall morning several years ago, we received a call from a San Diego Gas & Electric Company substation. A fox had become trapped inside a high-voltage area, sparks were flying everywhere, and they needed our help. Chuck, Michelle and Bruce, one of our male volunteers, headed out.

Upon arriving, they were greeted by six or eight burly linemen who had been trying to spook the fox from this very hazardous area. They thankfully greeted Chuck and Bruce and gave a pleasant nod to Michelle. The fox was definitely trapped in a very dangerous area, they explained, and their efforts in extracting him had been futile.

Chuck scoped out the situation and realized that none of our gear would work in this case and that someone with small hands would have to handle the fox. This nixed Chuck, Bruce and all the linemen. There stood little Michelle, ready to do the task at hand. Chuck got the carrier in position, Michelle donned the mammal gloves, and her audience held its collective breath. She reported later that she had held hers, too! She adroitly reached down, grabbed the fox's tail and in two seconds had him in the carrier! Everyone jointly exhaled. The linemen, to a man, began applauding Michelle's efforts. They were duly impressed.

Chuck, although equally impressed with Michelle, let the guys know that this was just routine for us and told them to call us if they ever needed our help again. Michelle did not cry this time. She did, however, grow about a foot taller. The fox was soon released in his native area, smart enough—we hope—to stay away from the substation.

In 1993, several years after this incident, SDG&E donated thousands of dollars worth of manpower, equipment and supplies toward the construction of our enormous, state-of-the-art rehabilitative flight cage. I firmly believe that this dream that became a reality would not have happened had Michelle been any less capable than she was on "The Day of the Fox." Oh, they may have remembered for a couple of days the attractive young woman who tried but failed to rescue the fox. In actuality, what they saw that day was a trained professional doing her job well—and successfully; that's what they remembered.

As hard as we try, we can't seem to teach the wildlife about human holidays. After all these years, they still have the nerve to become ill or injured while we humans are attempting to celebrate something. In fact, we generally receive more calls on holidays regarding ill or injured wildlife. This is due to the fact that more people are home, relaxing and observing more of their outside environment than they normally would be. Consequently, we are fully staffed on holidays. Our paid staff and committed volunteers are on duty if it's a day of the week that they should be here. As our consolation prize to

Because They Matter

those staff and volunteers who spend their holidays with us, Chuck and I try to send them home early. We allow them to arrive as early as they want, take care of our wildlife clientele, and once the necessary maintenance is done, barring emergencies, everyone may leave.

It was Thanksgiving 1992, and everyone had left for the day except for Michelle, who was deeply involved in a discussion with Chuck regarding native plants—what else. The topic was laurel sumac, and they were engrossed in their rantings of its benefits to the wildlife. The phone rang, and I, bored out of my mind by these two, gratefully answered the call. There was an injured duck on a pond several miles from us. People who regularly feed ducks at this pond had attempted to capture the injured one but hadn't been able to do so. The duck could fly, we learned, but had a spear of some sort sticking through its neck. Chuck gathered his net gun and Michelle and headed for the pond.

Sure enough, there was a beautiful mallard cruising the pond with a wooden spear about ten inches long completely through his neck. As luck would have it, the duck paddled to the shore at one point, and Chuck, using the net gun, was able to capture the mallard.

The wooden spear was a typical barbecue skewer with which some sick human had managed to gore this semi-domesticated duck. Proud of themselves and pleased with the fact that despite the hideousness of the situation, the duck looked all right and, barring something unforeseen, would probably do fine after surgery to remove the skewer, followed by some cage rest.

As Chuck, Michelle and their patient were preparing to leave, one of the onlookers stopped Chuck and pointed to the middle of the pond. There, swimming calmly, was a large white duck with a skewer sticking completely through her head. Someone had apparently fashioned themselves a home-made bow and arrow set and was shooting these mostly tame, trusting little creatures. This duck had sought the security of the tules in the pond and wasn't about to leave despite everyone's efforts.

Chuck refitted his net gun with floaters, and Michelle began wading into the pond to move the duck from the tules. The duck wasn't going to move, making it impossible for Chuck to get a clear shot. As Michelle moved closer, the duck began to frantically move away. Michelle knew she had to act quickly or lose the duck. In a last-ditch effort to evade Michelle, the duck made a swift dive underwater. Michelle followed suit.

What then ensued was the age-old story of the man versus the beast in the briny deep. In this saga, however, the man is a woman, the beast is a little white duck, and the briny deep is a three-foot pond. Within a few seconds Michelle reappeared, dripping with pond scum and holding the duck in her arms. A rousing cheer rose from the four bystanders and Chuck as the "swamp thing" and the duck emerged from the pond.

The swamp thing was crying and, unfortunately, one of the bystanders was a newspaper photojournalist. He asked Michelle for a quick photo and indicated that he would call the facility later for the story. A normally very photogenic Michelle agreed to pose while holding the duck for one quick

Because They Matter

shot, and the reporter did call later for the full story. In the meantime, Chuck, Michelle and the ducks headed home. The skewers were safely removed from both ducks. They were immediately placed on antibiotics as a precaution, and after two weeks of recuperation the ducks were released to a lovely, protected pond.

The sad part of this story came the day after the dramatic rescue, in the largest newspaper in San Diego County. Publicity for our work is very important as it lets people know that we are here to help the wildlife, so we were very pleased at the excellent article about the duck rescue.

The accompanying photo, however, put us into fits of laughter despite the tragedy of the situation. The entire photo consisted of the speared duck and Michelle's nostrils. This was to be Michelle's claim to fame after her daring escapade —a shot of her nose holes, embarrassingly enough identified in the paper as belonging to Michelle Lyons. She quit crying after a few days, and we were finally able to make fun of her to her face rather than behind it.

Michelle's 90-year-old Amachi (grandmother) cherishes family photos and often borrows photos from the homes of her grandchildren. She has yet to borrow the now-infamous nostril shot of her lovely granddaughter. Michelle has since gone on to bigger and better. In one very dramatic photo that appeared in the same newspaper several years later, an extremely professional-looking Michelle is shown holding our tranquilizer gun and standing over a very sleepy mountain lion. Chuck had tranquilized for relocation a mountain lion who had ventured too close to civilization. The photo taken of

Michelle and the lion was great—a wildlife rehabber's dream. Unfortunately, the caption underneath identified Michelle as me. I got a lot of praise for a job I didn't do, and Michelle got none. At least she didn't cry this time. Incidentally, the lion was released within its home range but farther away from suburbia.

On slow days, Michelle and Chuck like to go in search of "habitat." To Michelle, habitat means the native plants in a given area that support certain species. To Chuck, habitat means a given area that will support certain wildlife. He determines this by animal tracks and scat. In other words, if he finds an animal's footprints and its poop, then he knows that the given area is suitable for that animal. If he finds an overabundance of either, then the area may be too populated. On a good day, he and Michelle will discover a moderate amount of his and an abundance of her supportive vegetation. This is one of the ways we choose our release sites for those wild animals who have no established territory.

On one particular day, Michelle and Chuck headed out in opposite directions in the wilderness in their respective searches. Chuck was dissecting scat with his stick to discover the digested forms of Michelle's plants. Michelle was busy perusing the toyen, sumac, manzanita and God knows what else. A sudden rustling in the chaparral caught her off guard and she looked up. A beautiful coyote was tearing through the brush, stopping every few feet to look behind.

The coyote got within ten feet of Michelle, who was completely unperturbed. At one point, after stopping and checking his rear flank, the coyote made a mad frantic dash past Michelle and flung himself into the river below and began swimming across as if his life depended on it.

After this mesmerizing incident, Michelle turned around to the direction in which the coyote had been looking while he ran. Six black heads were barely visible above the brush. Michelle could tell that they were moving quickly toward her. She didn't know what they were until they began barking. They were a pack of feral dogs, far more dangerous than any wild animal we deal with. And they were coming for her, since they had lost the coyote. Michelle began screaming for Chuck—*and screaming for Chuck*—who ran toward her voice as quickly as he could.

Seconds later (which seemed like hours to Michelle), Chuck found her perched high in a tree and six large black dogs running back in the direction from which they came. Michelle's complexion was ashen as she looked down at Chuck from her haven in the tree. He assured her that she could come down, the dogs were gone.

They looked at each other and both realized that the getting down was not going to be as easy as the getting up had been. The first branch on Michelle's scrawny tree was about ten feet up, and that's where she was—there were no footholds or smaller branches to facilitate her coming down. As for her getting up there in the first place, we have all unequivocally decided that she sprouted wings and flew.

We have no other explanation, and Michelle simply remembers suddenly being there. With some finagling and a great deal of effort, Chuck got her out of the tree and safely back to us.

The part I find interesting is that Michelle was not upset by the coyote's presence, as he was where he belonged. The unnatural part was the feral dogs. Fortunately, Michelle was equipped with the knowledge to realize the dangers, and flew accordingly.

Michelle did not cry at this incident, much to our relief. However, her complexion remained rather pasty for several days. She has yet to show us those cute little wings she keeps tucked away somewhere.

Michelle is not the only one of us who cries. We all do at one time or another.

On one particularly tough day, Chuck, Michelle and I, with no one else around, found ourselves angry, frustrated and crying together. We had already lost a couple of animals that day due to the severity of their injuries.

Keeping our emotions in check, we grimly accepted a nine-week-old coyote pup from a woman. Her husband had shot it that morning, and in her words, "The darn thing wouldn't die."

She brought it to us simply to remove it from her property, as it was attracting the crows and ravens, who were, apparently in her mind, equal in their dastardliness to the coyotes. It never ceases to amaze me that people move to rural

Because They Matter

areas to "get away from it all" and are highly disturbed to find that wild animals actually live there!

The coyote pup was in bad shape. The bullet wound was compounded by severe dehydration and shock. The three of us worked quickly to help him, but it was too late. The pup died about ten minutes into our efforts. He was just a baby, and his death was just one too many that day, and we all cried.

Michelle does equally well with happy tears, and these are my personal favorites. Michelle was not with us in the early, very tough years of rescuing feral goats from San Clemente Island. The whole operation was exhilarating, but the best part for me was caring for the orphaned or rejected babies. One of the finest experiences of my life has been bottle-feeding baby goats. They are pure, unmitigated joy in my opinion. I told this to Michelle after she joined us, and she was very envious as she adores the "babies" of any species. I assured her that baby goats were head and shoulders above any other species, but since our male goats were all castrated —"nah, nah, nah," she wouldn't bottle-feed any out here. Well, I was wrong.

We had three large, beautiful, uncastrated Spanish Andalusian males in a separate enclosure from the other sixty or so castrated males and nannies. We had not fixed them because they were older, and the surgery risks were greater. The enclosure was fairly small for these three billies, and we wanted to put them in the lovely pasture with the others.

We consulted Dr. Larry Catt, one of our large-animal vets, about surgery. He felt that he could safely take care of our "boys." We opted for the surgeries so that these billy goats could join the others. As predicted, the surgeries went well, and the three guys were soon with the "in crowd." One little thing we forgot to account for was the fact that for a while following castration, a male goat can still impregnate a female. *Whoooops!*

Five months later we noticed one of our nanny goats acting strangely. We watched her for a couple of hours before realizing that she was trying to give birth but having a hard time with it. We caught her, calmed her down, checked her over and realized that her baby was breech. She couldn't do it alone. Chuck, Michelle and I donned our surgical gloves and prepared to help. At this point, Michelle was a little teary-eyed but maintaining. I think she knew she was about to embark on the experience of a lifetime.

Chuck's hands were too large to help this tiny nanny goat, so he asked Michelle to help while I restrained and soothed the nanny. "Help" involved Michelle's hands reaching inside the birth canal and twisting the baby around so that she could be born properly. The babies' tiny hooves had become caught in the nanny's pelvis so Michelle had to be very careful in feeling her way into unseen territory. After about ten tears, much sweat and a lot of talking to herself, a baby's head appeared, quickly followed by the rest of the baby, which was quickly followed by another head and another baby.

Both babies were alive, and mama reached around to clean their faces and introduce them to the world. After having her face cleaned and taking her first breath, the first baby goat looked up at Michelle and said *"maaaa."* It was all over then. Michelle sobbed a bucketful, and I wasn't far behind

Because They Matter

her, although I had "been there, done that." The second baby did the same thing, and Michelle's life changed forever.

This mama goat was not one of the feral Spanish Andalusians, she was a domestic milk goat, part of a herd of thirty or so that had been confiscated by humane officers after finding that they were being severely neglected. Every goat from that group was extremely malnourished, and every nanny had severe mastitis, a bacterial infection of the udders caused by, among other things, unsanitary conditions.

When we first took these goats, the nannies' udders drug on the ground. I don't remember an abuse case that hurt me as much as watching these poor goats trying to walk and stumbling every few steps because their rear legs had become twisted in their udders.

Within a few months, after antibiotic treatments, beautiful, clean living conditions and top-quality food, the nans' udders went back to their normal size. The udders, however, were filled with fibrous tissue, making them useless as milk goats (which was of no concern to us) but also making it impossible for them to feed their babies. The milk would be meager and possibly unhealthy for the offspring. After two years of living with us, this nanny was as healthy as she would ever be, but she couldn't care for her babies.

After we settled down and stopped crying from our ordeal of giving birth to two baby goats, I gently nudged Michelle and said, "Your babies are hungry and you'd better get busy!"

This was her first realization that we were going to have to bottle-feed them. She was beside herself with joy. We left the babies with their mom just long enough to acquire the colostrum-rich goat milk we needed, along with goat-size bottles and nipples. By the time we returned, the babies were prancing around the pasture with mom and attempting to nurse not only from her but anything with udders, including Mombo, our old lady sheep, who stood patiently and let the young ones nurse.

We didn't even know whether Mombo had milk, but the babies seemed content. They also had to have our special milk, so Michelle and I fixed the bottles, scooped up the kids, and I walked her through her first feeding. She loved it, I loved it, and the kids really loved it. As their real mom was very nurturing, we decided to leave them with her and feed them in the pasture, so nanny could supervise. We fed these two all that day and kissed them good night.

Bright and early next morning, with our bottles in hand, we found not two baby goats but four! Another nanny had given birth in the wee hours without our help. We rounded up our four charges and fed them breakfast, which thrilled them to pieces.

By late afternoon, the babies had already gotten used to the routine of feeding. We merely had to call "goaties" to summon our four charges. If we weren't fast enough, they'd nurse our knees, necks, elbows, or any other body part available. Michelle was in heaven, and life quickly became hell for Eric, her very patient husband.

From that day forward, Michelle pleaded with Eric to let her take the kids when they were older. Eric eventually agreed to let Michelle take the two little girls that she had "birthed," but not for several months. They had to be weaned, and Eric also had to construct a shelter and a fenced area on their property, just for "the girls." To his relief and ours, the anticipation of having her own baby goats quieted Michelle's pleading for a while.

The months passed, the kids were all weaned and just as attached to Michelle as they were their natural mother. Eventually the "girly-girls," as Michelle calls them, were safe and sound in their new home. Several months later, the other two kids somehow found their way to Eric and Michelle's house. It probably had something to do with a lot of tears and a good hot meal on the table every night when Eric got home from a hard day's work.

Nowadays, life is hard for Eric—he's lucky to have a cheese sandwich and a 7-Up waiting for him in the evening. The blame doesn't totally fall on the shoulders of Molly, Holly, Polly and Wally (her goat children) or Poncho and Cisco, their dogs, or Mr. K, the feral kitten who barged his way into their lives. In addition to her many years of working with us, Michelle is also working on her degree in biology at a local university. Her goal is to become a science teacher. With her compassion for all living beings, her knowledge of native wildlife and their habitats, and her moxie, Can-Do Michelle *will* do!

Michelle epitomizes the type of person who is so important to our work. She is courageous yet cautious, and constantly learning, both about the animals under our care and those in the wild. Her bravery, her tenacity, her knowledge and even her tears make her not only a fine wildlife rehabilitator but an educator.

On a personal note, this lovely Basque beauty is someone who has been through thick, thin, hideous and beautiful with me. She is my friend.

Bobby and Sugar

Bobby and Sugar were two tamed and imprinted adult bobcats who came to us courtesy of the California Department of Fish and Game. Bobby and Sugar had been confiscated when their "owners" attempted to enter California with them. It is illegal in California—as it should be in all fifty states—to possess any native wild mammal or bird as a pet.

Our previous experience with adult bobcats had been only with truly wild ones who were injured. Consequently, these two tamed ones had us mesmerized. They were like monstrously overgrown house cats, both in their behavior and looks. Although weighing in only at twelve and nine pounds respectively, Bobby and Sugar looked so much larger than house cats of the same weight. They played with each other, fought with each other and slept entwined in one another's arms.

Their records indicated that they were fourth-generation captive-raised bobcats from Oregon. Bobby was three years old, and Sugar was several months younger. They were both "intact," with claws on all four feet and all of their reproductive organs (although with Bobby, it was difficult to tell, as the male wild felids have very small testicles, unlike their domestic cousins).

We were given a certain period of time to "wild these critters up," as mandated by the Fish and Game officials, to prepare them for release. In our innocence we were prepared to do this, since the alternatives were either euthanasia or the location of an acceptable zoo to permanently house them. We felt that neither option was viable nor desired, so we became determined to ready them for release. This was much more difficult than anticipated, because these cats had a tendency to rub up against our legs or jump on our shoulders and rub our faces each time we entered their enclosure. At these times, never once were their claws protracted. They knew to be careful around humans.

We enjoyed them for the first few weeks. We freely entered their enclosure, caressed them and were in turn caressed by them. At some point, we decided no more of this—it's time to "wild them up."

For months we discouraged their affection and entered their enclosure only to clean it or to feed them. In the meantime, Chuck checked with every rehabilitation center in the country to see if anyone had successfully rehabbed and released bobcats who came from a situation similar to Bobby and Sugar's. He was unable to find anyone who had accomplished this. We became disheartened, but as we so often do in a job like this, we just took things one day at a time.

Bobby and Sugar continued their romance and seemed quite content with us. Bobby so loved Sugar and, apparently as a show of affection, he would suck on her little bobbed tail. Poor Sugar had to go through life with this soggy appendage drooping from her rear end. It was cute, but I have often wondered if this wasn't an indication of neurotic behavior on Bobby's part. Although captive-bred and raised, I can't help think that somewhere deep inside these cats, there was a yearning to be wild and free. People who raise wild animals as pets only

Because They Matter

succeed in stripping these animals of their dignity, but the wild instincts can never be taken away.

Early one spring, we noticed that Sugar had gained some weight. Thoughts of pregnancy did not really come to mind, although they should have. In early April, Sugar gave birth to three kittens. We were able to catch glimpses of them, and they were exquisite, miniature bobcats. Sugar was a good mother, rarely leaving them alone. We even put her food in the shelter with her, since she was reluctant to leave her babies, even to eat. By the third day, Sugar had no more babies.

As we discovered later, male bobcats do not assist in caring for babies and will often eat them. This was apparently the case with Sugar's babies. We were upset with ourselves for allowing this to happen, yet spaying and neutering Bobby and Sugar had been out of the question as long as we held any hope that they could be released into the wild.

Several months later, to our complete surprise, Sugar had three more babies. Both of these pregnancies occurred during the "wilding up" process. I discovered this one afternoon when I was alone at our center. I was doing a routine check of everyone and couldn't find Sugar.

From outside their enclosure, I was able to use a long stick to open the flap door to her shelter. It was then that I saw her with three tiny ones cuddled against her belly. There was no way I could enter their enclosure without risking my life, yet I knew I had to take these babies before we had a repeat incident. Using my long stick in one hand to reach through the chain link and push open the shelter door, I was able to use our snake grasper to pull out the babies one at a time.

Sugar didn't protest—maybe she was relieved. I scooped up the babies and rushed them to our medical center, got them on heat and prepared a formula. They were newborns and had nursed from Sugar very briefly, if at all. This meant that they might not have received that precious colostrum from Sugar's milk.

For three days and three nights we fed the babies every two hours. On the fourth day all three babies died. Despite all our efforts, nothing can compare to a natural mother's milk.

It was after these two tragic experiences that we realized Bobby and Sugar were not going to be able to be rehabbed for release into the wild. We immediately had them altered. All through these trying times, Bobby and Sugar had each other and obviously and truly loved one another.

Over the years we have watched dozens of wild bobcats under our care interact with one another and have seen our many domestic cats in their wishy-washy relationships with each other. Nothing we have seen can compare to the true devotion Bobby and Sugar had for each other. Sugar's little tail stayed soggy for weeks at a time, and she didn't seem to mind at all.

Because Bobby and Sugar were two little strangers in a strange land, creatures torn between the wild and domestic worlds, who only had each other, I often thought that should one die, the other would follow soon after. Only time will tell, as this story does have a happy ending.

I do not approve of zoos in general, because I feel that in most cases the zoo animals are merely goods to be bought, sold and exploited at will. However, on numerous occasions we were called regarding injured wildlife by The Living Desert Museum in Palm Desert, just a couple of hours from us.

We would either pick up, or they would transport to us, injured native wildlife that had come to them. We were impressed by the caring and concern for animals shown by everyone we met—the director, her staff and the keepers themselves.

During several visits there, we learned that construction was almost complete on a lovely series of habitats called Eagle Canyon. We were invited for a behind-the-scenes tour and found it most impressive. The areas where specific animals were to be kept were truly in keeping with natural habitat in the wild. We concluded that for any wild animal doomed to a captive life, Eagle Canyon would be a nice home.

We approached museum director Terry Correll regarding Bobby and Sugar, as we knew that they were constructing a bobcat habitat. Terry was more than willing to accept our cats, and we were elated. The habitat has a sand floor complete with rocks and mountainous outcroppings to form the walls of the enclosure. Planter boxes were built in the walls to allow for some native plants to be included in the exhibit. A Plexiglas viewing window would allow visitors to see the bobcats.

The day finally came for Bobby and Sugar to leave us for their new home. Kim Worrell from the museum drove to pick them up. Kim would be Bobby and Sugar's keeper and was as excited as we were. We readied two carriers for the trip, planning to put one cat in each carrier. We had our tranquilization equipment ready just in case one or both of the cats happened to be a little cranky and not ready for a road trip.

With wild animals, even "domesticated" ones, their behavior can never be predicted. We placed one carrier in their enclosure, opened the gate and crossed our fingers. Much to our surprise, Bobby stepped into the carrier and sat down; within two seconds, Sugar followed. God, that was easy—we were so relieved. We quickly closed the gate before they could change their minds. Obviously these two were not going to allow themselves to be separated for any reason.

Kim transported them to their new home, and from all reports (and our own visits) they are doing very well. From what we hear, Bobby will not allow any of the lovely native plants to flourish. He climbs the rocks and tears up all the flora in his habitat. Well, at least he's having fun, and he's not sucking Sugar's tail anymore. He apparently has better things to do now.

Bobby and Sugar are loved by all involved with them and have the visitors captivated by their antics and by their obvious love for each other. The latest photo we received from Kim shows Bobby and Sugar asleep in the sunshine, so entwined in each other that it is hard to tell where Bobby ends and Sugar begins!

Because They Matter

In the wild, bobcats are normally polygamous. This does not mean they lack the capacity to love or to be monogamous; life in the wild is so difficult (for so many reasons) that they must be opportunistic procreators in order to preserve their species.

I firmly believe that bobcats and other wild mammals and birds have a deep capacity for love of each other, and if given the chance would be monogamous. These are truly sentient beings with the ability to love, and to be cranky at times.

Bobby and Sugar opened so many doors for us in terms of observation of bobcats. In so many ways they were wild and behaved accordingly, giving us great insight into bobcat behavior. Yet in so many other ways they were misfits in both the wild and domestic worlds.

Regardless of what we learned or didn't learn, these two lovely beings love each other deeply and will remain together until the end. Isn't that a great lesson for human beings to learn?

The Red-Tail with an Attitude

Most visitors to our wildlife rehabilitation center are more mesmerized by our birds of prey than by any other animals under our care. Part of this is due to the beauty and design of our large rehabilitative flight cage and, of course, part is due to the sheer majesty of the birds themselves.

We have dealt with and observed literally thousands of ill, injured or orphaned birds of prey at our center and, frankly, I haven't seen much in the way of a personality in most of them. I am much more impressed by the little wild finches, sparrows and other songbirds we care for here.

Birds of prey—vultures, hawks, owls, eagles and falcons —are, by necessity, I admit, eating machines. Except for brief mating periods, their entire lives are spent either hunting for or eating their carnivorous diet—their very survival depends on this. Consequently, because they are so busy just trying to survive, there is little room or time for development of endearing personalities.

All baby animals are beautiful, including baby birds of prey, and for a short while, when the babies are reliant on us for food, they have wonderful and distinct personalities. In every grouping, there's always a shy one, one slower to mature, one who appreciates you and one who absolutely hates your guts. Had this grouping remained in the wild, the last one mentioned would probably be the only one to survive beyond its first year. Life is very tough, and only the strong survive out there.

Spring of 1991 was very busy for us and all of our fellow rehabbers. We were all overloaded with wild babies of all species, including birds of prey. No animal needed to be raised alone. We traded baby birds of prey like they were baseball cards. Donna Barron and Nancy Conney, raptor experts with Project Wildlife, a sister organization in San Diego County, got our first kestrel falcon and great horned owlet, since they already had several of each. We got their first barn owlet, as we had acquired two others previously.

We all did this mixing and matching to ensure that each baby raptor would be raised with its own kind. By the middle of baby season, we didn't have to mix and match anymore. We all had dozens of every species. Babies would be raised wild and free of unnecessary human contact and would do well in the wild.

There was, however, one lone holdout, a licensed rehabber who raised one solitary red-tailed baby hawk. Not only did she not attempt to locate someone with similar babies, she allowed her husband, a teacher, to use this very impressionable baby as an educational tool in his classroom. She called us in late fall of 1991 to "borrow" space in our large flight cage for this now "teenage" red-tailed hawk.

She was a beautiful teenager, a well-fed and "exquisite specimen" when she came to us, and totally imprinted on humans. Once we verified she would eat our staple diet for birds of prey, we moved her to our large flight cage, hoping that the companionship of other red-tailed hawks would help her mature. The danger with an "imprint" is that they do not have the innate fear of humans that their wild counterparts have.

Because They Matter

This bird was not tame and was, in fact, extremely aggressive toward humans. Sadly enough, her hawk companions in the flight cage did nothing to alter her personality for the better.

We pondered the fate of this beautiful female red-tailed hawk. We could keep her in our flight cage as a permanent resident, we could work with her to use her as an educational animal, or we could euthanize her. Setting her free with her existing behaviors was completely out of the question—she was dangerous to herself *and* others. We named her "The Witch," yet we were all very fond of her and truly felt pity for her situation.

After several months, her aggressiveness toward humans seemed to taper off and became directed toward her food. This was good. We became optimistic. She still had no fear of humans, yet neither was she as eager to approach us as she had been. A month grew into a year, and The Witch was pretty well-behaved, so no decision as to her fate had to be made immediate.

As she approached her second year, her adult red tail feathers began to emerge, one at a time. She still chirped like a baby but was rapidly becoming an adult. We all sensed her frustration as she flew back and forth across the fifty-foot span of the flight cage for hours. She wanted something more out of life than simply a cage. Our flight cage houses many types of hawks and owls. While not friendly with each other, they all manage to coexist quite well. The large size of the cage is one reason for this peaceful cohabitation. Another reason is that Chuck purposely overfeeds. No raptor has to get less than its fill every day. Consequently, it was odd for us to discover the Witch attempting to prey on other birds in the flight cage.

Hunting is an instinctual behavior in birds of prey. The Witch wanted to hunt, not because she had to, but because she *wanted* to. It was a compelling force within her. Although not her fault, this behavior could not exist in our flight cage. Our dilemma hit us in the face, and we had only two choices at that point: Euthanize her or set her free.

I sincerely felt that if we euthanized her, we were killing the victim of the crime and not the perpetrator. Chuck felt the same way and noted that if she became a problem—if we set her free—we could capture her and euthanize her then.

Our experience with raptors has been that if we release them on our property (their territory) and they have been under our care for an extended period of time, as The Witch had been, that they will stay here. With our fingers crossed, we set The Witch free in early 1993.

True to form, she stayed close by and was generally visible in one of our huge trees. She would come closer to us in late afternoons, when Chuck puts out food for many of our former residents.

At about four o'clock she would land on one of our thirty-foot power poles and "chirp" incessantly for the food with which she had become familiar while under our care. She was no problem to us at all and behaved very well.

She proved to be an excellent huntress, exhibiting only one facet of her captive personality: She hunted the squirrels, gophers and field mice on our property, not caring that we were standing only a few feet away. She continued to have no fear of humans, yet she also knew that we humans were not her source for food. She had found her own, albeit right under our eyes.

The good part was that she stayed right here. The bad part was that we watched her eat other animals whose lives mattered just as much to them as her life mattered to her. It's often not easy accepting the predator-prey relationship that exists in nature, but we are fools if we don't.

We saw The Witch daily, and she was beautiful—always looking well fed yet always eager for another morsel from Chuck. She was a full adult, thrilled with her independence from us yet always checking in with us every afternoon. So strong, brave and aggressive was she, and we were proud of her and her adjustment into the real world. With spring of 1994 just a few months away, we were eager to see if she would, or could, accept a mate and do normal "red-tail things."

Early one Monday morning in December of 1993, everything changed for us and The Witch. An irate Ramona resident drove up our driveway to report an injured hawk about fifty feet from our entrance. Chuck rushed down to care for the injured hawk, only to discover that it was The Witch. She had a badly broken leg. The woman who found her was furious because she had seen a fellow motorist purposely swerve to hit her while she was eating a freshly caught squirrel on the side of the road. We were furious, too, but more distraught than angry. We had brought this lovely creature such a long way on the road to freedom only to have it all snatched away from her. If the fracture couldn't be repaired, we would have no choice but to euthanize her. One-legged raptors cannot survive in the wild or in captivity.

Much to our joy, the fracture was simple and clean. Dr. Don Wood was able to insert a pin in her leg to allow her fracture to mend properly. The Witch was taken to our medical center for a month of recuperation. She healed beautifully and was soon ready for a few weeks of muscle-building in a flight enclosure.

By this time, late January 1994, our new 150-foot free-flight enclosure was in use, and its sole occupants were three juvenile golden eagles we were preparing for release. Our brainstorm at this point was to put Witchie-poo in with the eagles. As they were larger, she'd probably make no attempts on their lives. Our ulterior motive was that since Witchie-poo was an accomplished huntress, she could probably teach these gangly, slow-moving teenage eagles a little something about life in the wild and what they had to do in order to survive.

Weeks passed and Witchie-poo demonstrated her skills—too well, in fact—on numerous occasions. With great finesse, she successfully preyed on all the food put into the flight cage, even when it was far more than she herself could consume. Our lazy little eagles became accustomed to eating Witchie-poo's leftovers. They didn't have to hunt, she did it for them. Eagles will eat carrion and often prefer a nice road kill to something they have to chase to eat. Well, so much for that bright idea. It was time anyway to give Witchie-poo her freedom again.

While Witchie-poo had been in our hospital, we had released several juvenile red-tails who had come to us with various injuries. They all stayed around for several days before venturing out into the real world. Only one stayed behind and claimed our land as his territory. This was all well and good until time to re-release Witchie-poo. From the moment she was released, she worked on getting this juvenile off her land. The youngster was stubborn and not about to give up either. They'd bicker, have minor skirmishes and then apparently ignore each other. We also began ignoring them, as very natural things were taking place.

This drama continued for several months until one day in late June, I noticed Witchie-poo sitting outside the medical center door. She still had no fear of humans, so I assumed she was waiting for someone to feed her. We had long since stopped that practice, so I walked past her, ignored her and entered the medical center. I emerged about an hour later, and she was still sitting in the same spot. As I walked past her, I muttered to her that she'd better move along because I wasn't going to feed her.

Later that day, I headed back over to the medical center. Witchie-poo was still there, staring off into space. This time I stopped to look at her, as she had been there for hours. Her left eye was swollen and bloodied, and her head was covered with dried blood. The bird was hurt and had been trying all that time to check herself into the hospital!

My heart ached for her, yet at the same time, I marveled at her intelligence. She had five acres of property as her domain and could have stood anywhere on those five acres until someone found her. She chose to stand on the railing, two feet away from the door to the medical center. She knew exactly where to go for help. I donned my raptor gloves and carefully picked her up, took her inside and examined her injuries.

She had some pretty severe puncture wounds and was very depressed. Fortunately, her eye was fine, just swollen from a wound right above it. We cleaned her up, started her on a good antibiotic and set her up in the hospital. She did not eat the first day, which didn't surprise us. The next morning she was still severely depressed. She was hurting. We all began to be very concerned at this point. Our saucy, feisty red-tail seemed to have lost her will to live.

She refused all food for three days and threw up what we hand-fed her. Physically, she looked better. Her swollen eye was almost back to normal, yet her attitude was the pits. This loss of spunk could have killed her as much as her injuries. When an animal loses its will to live, nothing we humans can do will help that animal. We had healed her wounds; she had to heal her heart.

Every morning for a solid week, we expected to find her dead in the hospital. We didn't, however, and somehow during that week, she convinced herself that she wanted to live. After that awful seven days, we walked in on the eighth day to find a mad hawk jumping at the cage door and screaming. She had eaten all the food provided the day before and was screaming for more. At this point, our lives were in more

Because They Matter

danger than hers was. Now we had to deal with, on a daily basis, a mad, imprinted, recuperating red-tailed hawk.

Handling any bird of prey is difficult and should be done only by those well-trained in handling raptors. Handling an imprinted one with a bad "tude" is much worse. Witchie-poo knew our weak points, and despite our protective gear, a couple of us got nailed. She'd aim for arms exposed above our gloves or, better yet, our faces. She got a couple of us in the arm but missed our faces, fortunately. We are always cautious when handling any of our wildlife but have learned to be doubly alert when dealing with one that has no fear of humans.

Every time I handle a red-tail, I remember our gutsy friend Nancy Conney, with the raptor team of Project Wildlife. Nancy was holding a red-tail for their veterinarian, Rose Brown, to examine. While running her mouth (as she often does), Nancy loosened her restraint momentarily. The hawk, sensing that she was free, pulled a leg from Nancy's gloved hand and went for her mouth.

It took three people to pry this bird's talons from Nancy's upper lip and chin. She bears no scars from this ordeal, the hawk in question was soon released back into the wild, and we all learned a good lesson: Never let down your guard when dealing with a wild animal. We all know this, but sometimes it takes an incident to bring the point home.

Witchie-poo rapidly improved, and within a couple of weeks she was ready for a short stay in the flight cage prior to her release. By September of 1994, Witchie-poo was ready to try the real world one more time. We netted her in the big flight cage, carried her outside and gave her freedom again.

She's been free for several years now and seems to relish every moment. She's behaved herself this time and hasn't "kicked butt" or had her own butt kicked by any of the other neighborhood red-tails.

She checks in every afternoon, shrieking across the property and taking her position on a tall telephone pole. She's still provided with some food from us but hunts our fields with great finesse. She's a survivor and would supply the area with some magnificent genes should she ever mate. Although she has shown no amorous tendencies toward any other hawks, she has been seen flying with nesting material in her talons, so we know those instincts are intact. Will she or won't she? We don't know—we just hope.

Birds of prey have the potential for living well over twenty years. Witchie- poo will live every one of them with gusto, and maybe, somewhere down the road, she'll show up on our telephone pole one day with a couple of gawky little fledglings who only know her as "Mommie Dearest."

Leaping Lena

We have a neighbor who keeps a large "live trap" set on his property. He raises different types of fowl and pigeons that are threatened, not by the wildlife in our rural community, but by free-roaming dogs allowed to run loose by their careless owners. The dogs he catches are turned over to the Department of Animal Control. Many of his neighbors who have had to "bail out" their dogs have learned an expensive lesson.

Once in a while he catches an opossum or a skunk. In these cases he calls us. We retrieve the wildlife and bring them back to the center for a physical exam. If they're okay, we release them back in their home territory. A couple of years ago he trapped a coyote that appeared to be injured. We picked her up, brought her to the center and discovered that her injury was not new and had completely healed. She was missing about a quarter of her right foreleg, another one of those hideous steel-jaw-trap stories. She had chewed off her own foot to gain her precious freedom.

Speaking of steel-jaw traps, the "new wave" are the offset and padded ones, supposedly humane. They are all objects of torture. An animal caught in any one of these will attempt to escape at any cost. Anyone who uses any type of steel-jaw trap should be forced into using it on himself first, just to see how it feels. We have quite a confiscated collection here, as a matter of fact. We have removed domestic cats, foxes, coyotes and birds of prey from them.

While the mammals have managed to survive, maybe just

minus a toe, foot or leg, someone forgot to tell the birds of prey that these padded or offset traps are humane. Their legs are snapped like twigs, and the birds must be euthanized, as a one-legged raptor has no chance for survival. Enough of this and back to Lena.

In addition to her disability, Lena was extremely pregnant. It was early March (coyote pups are generally born in March), and we didn't know whether Lena had raised other pups with her disability. Raising healthy pups requires an enormous amount of energy and skill for a mama coyote. While nursing the pups, she must be able to feed herself in order to feed the pups. Later, she must be able to hunt, not just for herself but for her weaning pups. Part of mama coyote's weaning process is to regurgitate part of what she has eaten for her pups.

With this concern for Lena and her unborn pups, we decided to let her have her pups here. We put Lena in our large enclosure with Yote, our permanent-resident coyote. Once she had adjusted to captivity, with the assistance of Yote the peacemaker, Lena began digging a den. All of our enclosures have wire under the ground to prevent mammals from digging out. Our coyote enclosure is so large that we have wire only five feet inside the perimeter, leaving the center of the enclosure unwired. Lena dug her den in the center, about two feet down and with four feet of tunneling to ensure that her pups would be secluded and safe.

She disappeared one evening, so we knew it was time. She was denning, and what a temptation it was to check on her pups. None of us had seen newborn coyotes before. Good

Because They Matter

sense prevailed, and we left Lena and her pups alone. Chuck put her food right in her den every evening, consequently we didn't see Lena for several weeks, except for quick glimpses of her limping to the water tub for a sip of fresh water.

Despite her disability, that girl could move, thus the name Leaping Lena. She was a wonderful mother and watched her six pups carefully when they began to emerge from the den.

Yote was not the doting father figure we had hoped for with Lena's pups. If one strayed too far from Lena, he would snatch that pup and shake it like a rag doll. The ever-attentive Lena would become a dynamo at this point. She would tear into Yote and quickly retreat into her den with all six pups in

tow. Yote never hurt a pup, but the potential was certainly there, and Lena sensed it. Except for those rare occasions, Yote and Lena had a great relationship, full of coyote "I'll chase you and then you chase me" games.

As Lena's pups matured, they learned these games as well. To make a long story short, we released Lena and six healthy pups back into her home territory. The pups—not really pups anymore—were teenagers and old enough to fend for themselves if they had to do so. Coyote pups often remain with their mother into their second year and frequently help her raise the following year's litter of pups. We hoped that Lena and her pups would stay together, but we will never know.

It is estimated that about fifty percent of all wild animals born will not survive their first year. This heartbreaking thought weighs heavily on our minds when we release animals, especially the babies we have raised. However, we cannot question forces beyond our control. We can only do our best to prepare the animals for the "wild world" out there and hope they beat the odds.

In late November of the year following Lena's release, our "live trap" neighbor again called us. He had caught a coyote, possibly injured. It had been more than a year since we released Lena and her pups, but we hadn't forgotten that brave little mama coyote, and we all held our breaths on the quick drive over to the neighbor's house.

Glory be—it was Lena and we were excited! She looked very healthy. We had to act really blasé in front of our neighbor, however, as we have assured him that we release coyotes in remote areas where they won't "bother" humans again.

We "tsk-tsked" over this coyote that we pretended we didn't know, promised our neighbor that we'd fix her up and release her somewhere else. Lena had wanted a duck dinner, which she didn't get, and was lured into the live trap by canned cat food, a much easier meal to catch.

Our neighborhood was obviously her home. The area is very rural with plenty of wide-open spaces. Lena belongs here

Because They Matter

as much as, if not more than, we humans do. We brought her back to the center. Yote was happy to see his old friend. They chased and played for three or four days, and Lena chowed down at our famous restaurant.

We then released her "back home again." Apparently she has learned about live traps this second time around. We haven't seen her since, and it's been several years now. Lena's a survivor above all else, and we are confident that she's lost her appetite for duck dinner and canned cat food. We are equally confident that she's still out there somewhere.

Godspeed, Leaping Lena!

Beakers and Finchie-poo

Before our operation became so large that we were doing dozens of different species of orphaned songbirds a season, we often improvised by placing one species in with another species if we only had one of each.

Such was the case with little Finchie-poo, an orphaned finch, and Beakers, a badly injured baby meadowlark. Little Beakers (who was twice the size of the finch) had lost half of his beak to a lawn mower. Rather than euthanizing him immediately, we decided to watch him and see if he would be able to compensate for his disability.

Baby finches and meadowlarks are gentle little birds, so we put these two together so they wouldn't feel so alone in a strange place. As babies, their diet was the same, and they both eagerly gaped for food every hour on the hour, and in between meals snuggled together, peacefully asleep, in their little nest.

They grew by leaps and bounds and began using their legs and flapping their little pinfeathers. They became fledglings, with Beakers towering over Finchie-poo, but were still fast friends.

Feeding time became a frenzy, because in the nest, the squeaky wheel gets the grease. In other words, the most obnoxious, loudest and largest baby in the nest gets fed more often. These little orphans didn't realize that they would both be fed until their crops were full. (Nobody goes hungry with "Aunt Michelle" coordinating the diet and feeding schedule.)

Finchie-poo tried her darnedest to outgape, outchirp and to be taller than Beakers. She just couldn't do it. One day at feeding time, we were surprised to note that she had learned a new ploy to outsmart Beakers: She had jumped on his back, making herself much taller than he, and with this newfound self-confidence, she outchirped and outgaped him like a pro! In her little mind, she was the top dog!

This competition existed only at feeding time, however. Nap time would find these two perched side by side, fast asleep, sharing body heat and getting comfort from each other's presence.

As they flourished and grew older, the time came for what I refer to as "tough love"—the weaning process. At this stage, we extend the time between feedings and keep plenty of their natural diet available to them in their cage. Being a bird mommy is a tough job, as it's always hard to say "no" when a little fledgling is doing its finest dances to gain your attention.

Beakers, with Finchie-poo perched firmly on his shoulders, did dances to rival *Swan Lake* during this period of change. It was so hard to deny them food at these precious times, but we knew they would never know the joys of being wild and free if we didn't wean them.

They continued their beautiful little pliés every hour on the hour, but we quickly got wise to these two! Their cage diets began disappearing, yet these Siamese twins kept on dancing for us. They both made every effort not to let us catch them eating their natural foods. We would walk into the medical facility as quietly as possible to try to find out who was eating the natural diet. They heard us coming every time and

94   *Because They Matter*

were waltzing before we even entered the room. We had to find out, especially in Beakers' case, if he was capable of self-feeding. Like Peeping Toms, we began sneaking peeks in the windows of the nursery, walking from one window to the next, hoping to get a clear view. We finally found the best view and watched them for about ten minutes. Lo and behold, both of them were eating. What a thrill and a relief.

Beakers had over-come his disability and stood a good chance for making it now. Finchie-poo was do-ing very well also. Her only problem was that she had to dance and gape at her food before she ate it; con-sequently, while she was busy trying to get her food dish to feed her, Beakers was chowing down. We didn't want these two to feel completely abandoned now that we had caught them eating on their own, so we very gradually eliminated their hand-feeding schedule until they were no longer reliant on us for food.

Don't get me wrong, this weaning stage only meant that we were weaned from them—it did not mean that they would stop begging from us! We turned deaf ears and blind eyes to their finest performances.

After they were completely self-feeding for about ten days, we moved them to our outdoor aviary. This is where birds really learn that they are birds. Only natural diets are on the menu, and different species learn about coexistence with one another; it's a microcosm of life in the wild. Beakers and Finchie-poo stood open-mouthed for awhile, truly amazed at the world outside of their cage in the nursery.

After about three days, the beautiful tandem dances ended, and Finchie-poo began cavorting with other finches in the aviary. Both little birds seemed happy, were learning to fly and were almost ready to face the real world. After about two weeks, we determined that they were ready to leave us. Finchie-poo no longer danced, and Beakers seemed strong and healthy despite his disability.

On the assigned release morning, we found Finchie-poo rarin' to go. Little Beakers, however, was dead on the floor of the aviary. We released our little finch with some friends she had made, and she cheerfully left us to enjoy her new life.

We carefully examined Beakers' little body. He was well fed and healthy; there was no trauma or sign of disease. We can only speculate, as we didn't perform a necropsy, but we tend to think that Beakers knew better than us that his chances of survival in the wild were severely diminished because of his disability.

As we anthropomorphize so many of the wild mammals and birds we deal with, it's comforting (somewhat) for us to think that little Beakers, knowing instinctually that his time on the earth was limited, chose to die in the company of friends, rather than as some forgotten little carcass in an oat field.

These tiny little beings and their oneness with nature can teach us so much: little finches with their joy of life, dancing

Because They Matter

and spunk, living just for the moment, and sweet-voiced little meadowlarks, who turn the solitude of country life into a symphony hall.

The Egg

Early one April morning we received a call from a man who, while chopping down a tree for firewood, had discovered a nest of hatchling barn owls, along with an egg. Since it was too late to do our lecture on not trimming trees in the spring when birds are nesting, we asked him to bring the babies to our wildlife center. He asked if he should bring the egg also, since it was still intact. We encouraged him to do so, although we knew that the chances of the egg hatching were pretty slim.

Hungry babies, ranging in age from about four to seven days, and the egg arrived soon. We fed the babies and prepared to put them away for the afternoon. As an afterthought we tucked the tiny little egg in among the babies.

Several hours later, staffer Suzy Phillips and I had to disturb their nap to give them another feeding and to check on the egg. The egg was warm, and upon examination we saw a small hole beginning to form. Inside the hole, we could see a tiny heart beating. My God, The Egg was alive! Suzy and I looked at each other and at The Egg in wonder. Could we or should we help it? We didn't know, so "when in doubt, do nothing" became our motto. We tucked The Egg away again and finished our work for the day.

At sunrise the next day, I rushed over to the medical center to check on the status of our little charges and Egg. When I peeked in, I saw only half an eggshell where the whole egg had been the night before, and nothing else but the four hand-size, fuzzy, baby barn owls sound asleep in a tight little bunch. I carefully moved them aside and found, to my complete amazement, a fuzzy, thumb-size barn owl huddled and hidden by his (her?) siblings. That Egg had become somebody! I looked at this little being with my mouth hanging open in complete disbelief. He (she?) was perfectly formed, yet so small!

All of our staff fell utterly in love with the tiny being and were determined to keep this little fighter alive. We gently hand-fed him for several days, propping up his wobbly baby-head and carefully putting food in his mouth. He ate with gusto and by day four was strong enough to join his siblings for what we called the "pizza party." We placed all the food for one meal on a large plate and put the baby owls around the plate. They bobbed and wobbled, and eventually one would find the food. Once one did, the others would quickly follow suit.

Egg could bob and wobble like a pro but would land face down in the food. We would often lift his silly face from the dish to help him out and be met with squawks of complaint. He liked his face in the food and always managed to get his fair share that way. Egg grew rapidly and became every bit the barn owl as his siblings. He carried himself well and soon held his own with his huge brothers and/or sisters. Egg, with his zest for life, also proved himself to be a great teacher. When he was about a week old, we took in another hatchling barn owl from our friends at Project Wildlife.

P.W., as we called this owl, was bigger than Egg (although that wasn't saying much) yet smaller than Egg's sib-

Because They Matter

lings, and didn't have a clue what to do at the "pizza party." P.W. would just stand around the plate, bobbing and weaving and looking at Egg with squinty eyes of amazement. Egg would squawk, bob, wobble, fall in the food dish and come up with a lovely luncheon morsel and glare back at poor P.W., who would just stand there. An angry Egg would then repeat his motions, glaring deeper and squawking louder.

Eventually P.W. got the idea and copied Egg's movements. He was one hungry owl and bobbed, wobbled and ate till he could eat no more. Two thumbs up for Egg and P.W.!

The joy we felt from watching Egg thrive was enormous. Eventually he and his siblings and goofy P.W. were "graduated" to the large flight cage to become *real* barn owls and were released into the wild that summer.

Our joy, however, was tempered by a couple of facts that we as wildlife rehabilitators must deal with almost on a daily basis. First, if Egg's family had not been disrupted, neither Egg nor at least one of his siblings would have lived beyond a week. A mother owl can only do so much, and with a clutch of eggs hatching several days apart, only the first few hatched and the strongest will get the food; the others often become food. This is nature's way, but we were forced to interfere.

The second concern we have is that by ensuring the survival of the entire clutch, rather than half of it, are we propagating a weaker gene pool? These are fears and concerns of all of us who deal with wildlife under unusual circumstances.

We do the best we can, focusing on each individual and its instincts and will to survive. I will not judge the animals or question nature's way. I only look at Egg, who became a living being virtually before my eyes. In his mind and in his beautiful barn owl heart, he was the first-born, the strongest, and the one destined to make it. Maybe Mother Nature made a mistake just this once!

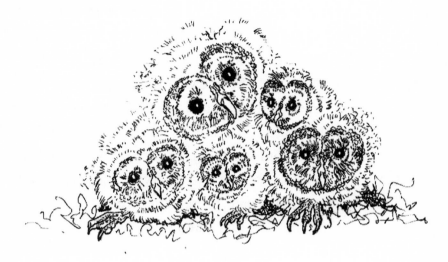

Baby Bob

This little wildling came to us after hikers had found him huddled under some chaparral. We will never know whether his mother had abandoned him, had gotten killed or was just out searching for food. All too often, wild babies are assumed to be "orphans" when, in fact, they aren't. Regardless of this, we had a week-old bobcat kitten on our hands.

He was probably the most exquisite creature I had ever seen. His claws were phenomenal, even at that early age. We had to wrap him in a towel to bottle-feed him, for our own protection. Bobcat claws are razor sharp, allowing these wild cats to slice or claw. This baby was no exception and would flail and claw the air at feeding time. Occasionally a claw would land on a human hand, drawing blood immediately.

The little distinctive bobcat tail was about three-quarters of an inch long on our little monster, and when he became angry (even at a week old) his little stub would twitch furiously. We all took turns bottle-feeding him to give our various wounds a chance to heal.

Mercifully, within two weeks he was ready to begin the weaning process. I realized he was ready when he viciously ripped the rubber nipple off his bottle one morning. His first meal was a slurry, comprised mainly of Gerber's chicken and other puréed meats. He took to it immediately.

Bobcat kits are much easier to wean than their domestic cousins. Life in the wild is rough, and babies have to mature quickly in order to survive.

Baby Bob loved his slurry and would dive into it with his face and all fours. This dining experience always called for a bath afterward, as these babies must be kept clean to prevent a multitude of problems from occurring.

Bathing any cat is a nightmare. Consequently, bathing a little bobcat is not one of life's greatest pleasures. He kicked, screamed, clawed and twitched his stubby tail throughout the entire ordeal. This was not great fun for all concerned. Much to our pleasure, he quickly graduated to whole meats instead of mush, so the bathing ritual ended. He also began grooming himself, much to our relief.

I love cats and have raised many orphaned domestic kittens. Raising this little wild cat was fascinating; the wild ones are so much like their domestic cousins yet so different. There

was to be no cuddling or nuzzling of Baby Bob. As with all wild babies, we have to keep them wild. He was attached to us in the sense that he knew we brought food, but this would pass as he grew up, went to the outdoor enclosure and did not see where his food came from.

Baby Bob had a terrible habit of purring when he saw us, sparking the maternal instincts in all of us. This was a lonely

Because They Matter

little baby who needed someone. The urge to cuddle him at these times was tremendous, yet we had to resist. We have seen too many beautiful wild animals ruined by being raised incorrectly.

Shrinking habitat for wildlife is a tremendous problem in California, and wildlife are forced into becoming "urbanized" in order to survive. However, this urbanization of the wild ones does not mean that they should trust, depend on or approach humans for food. Our job is to see that the orphaned wild babies we care for are released back into the wild with the same degree of wariness of humans as their raised-in-the-wild counterparts.

In order for us to ensure that Baby Bob knew he was a bobcat, it became very important, at this stage of his development, that he be raised with other bobcat kittens. Orphaned bobcats are generally few and far between, as female bobcats are very good mothers and as a rule do not abandon healthy kittens. Nevertheless, we put out our feelers with local wildlife groups that we had a baby bobcat who needed companionship.

Within a few days we received word from Project Wildlife and Wildlife Rescue that each group had a baby bobcat. Helen Cramer, the bobcat pro with Project Wildlife, had taken in a pretty weak baby. Wildlife Rescue had taken in one that was slightly older but orphaned for some reason, most likely because he just strayed too far from mom after reaching that "curious stage."

Both of those groups were eager for all three babies to be raised together. We happened to have an enclosure available that would be suitable for the little bobcats, so we were allowed the honor of raising these three. Helen's weak little female had done well under her care, our Baby Bob was fat and rambunctious, and Wildlife Rescue's slightly older male was very healthy.

All baby mammals acquire their initial immune system from the colostrum in their mother's milk. Babies that don't nurse from their mothers, either at all or not long enough, are prone to diseases they would normally be protected from had they nursed. Generally, we keep newcomers separate from any others until we can be sure, either through blood work or with a quarantine period, that the new baby isn't incubating a disease.

In the case of our three little bobcats, we were so eager for them to be together that we immediately commingled them. This was not entirely a foolhardy decision, since all three had been in quarantine already. Baby Bob had been with us for several weeks. Little Girl Bob had been with Helen, and Older Bob had been under Wildlife Rescue's care.

The three had a large room to themselves and became immediate and fast friends. Baby Bob pounced on Little Girl Bob and pounced on Older Bob. They pounced back and did very silly wild-kitten things that few humans get to observe. The door to their room has a viewing window, so we were able to watch these little orphans, with no mother cat to guide them, make up their own game rules as they learned stalking, hiding and pretend-hunting techniques.

They would do all the things domestic kittens do in play, but for these babies, their play was no game. They had to develop these skills to perfection in order to survive in their wild world. So these three babies clumsily attempted to teach each other the necessary survival skills.

I can remember peeking through their window on many occasions, watching them play, only to have a huge lump in my throat and a few tears on my face. At these times I fought the urge to enter their room, scoop them up and tame them while they were still young enough. The wild world is so hard on them, and life expectancies of animals in the wild are much shorter than animals kept in captivity. Every day I tell myself that these are wild animals, meant to be in the wild, and how unblessed our lives would be if we were not able to catch brief glimpses of these elusive creatures in our wilderness areas.

To put my mind in its proper perspective, I make myself think of two things. First: quality of life versus quantity of life; I would rather spend a few years of absolute freedom and joy than many years in a cage. Second: I think about Striker's eyes.

Striker is a bobcat who was found in the high-desert area, wandering aimlessly and close to death from malnutrition. Only after getting him to our center and giving him a physical examination did we discover that he had been surgically declawed—not just his front feet, but all four feet. He had been someone's "pet." Apparently, whoever had him grew tired of him and abandoned him in the desert. A despicable thing for a human being to do to any animal.

About a year old at the time, Striker recovered quickly and doubled his weight in two months. He is a lovely, healthy cat now. He is also a physically and mentally maimed wild animal who will never know freedom. When I look in his face, I see a faraway look in his eyes. He never looks *at* me, he looks beyond me, and I know that his thoughts are far beyond the confines of his captive world. He is longing for a world he has not known and will never know.

Baby Bob and friends were almost old enough for an outdoor enclosure. They were eating all of the food that was presented to them and rapidly becoming real bobcats.

One evening when I went to feed them, I noticed that Baby Bob was not as eager to eat as he usually was. He snatched the food, sniffed it but did not eat.

The other two kittens were as eager as usual. I also noticed some odd stains on their bedding. The stains appeared to be vomit. I was disturbed, but seeing that all three had been the picture of health just a few hours earlier, I wasn't too alarmed.

By the next morning, Baby Bob was severely depressed and dehydrated. Unsure of what could bring him down so quickly, we rushed him to Dr. Don Wood, our veterinarian. The diagnosis was panleukopenia (feline distemper), one of those dastardly cat diseases that can kill a kitten in a matter of hours.

Dr. Wood hooked up Baby Bob to a slow-drip IV of lactated Ringer's to help with the dehydration and electrolyte imbalance. We also put him on a heating blanket.

Baby Bob was basically comatose, yet all the while this wonderful, brave little baby was purring. I put my hands on his face and stroked him. I wanted him to know that his "mom" was with him. He continued purring for a few more moments, then quietly slipped away from this world.

The next day, Little Girl Bob also passed away. We were grief-stricken at the loss of these kittens and worried about Older Bob as well. He never became ill and grew into a lovely juvenile bobcat. The following spring we released him, along with three other juveniles who came to us that summer.

All of this was a learning process for those of us involved with these kittens. We can all clinically study our successes and failures with these babies and gain something for the future. From the emotional point of view, I will always re- member our little baby "bobs" trying so hard to be tough; teaching each other bobcat games with no adult to guide them. Beautiful, brave baby bobcats running wild and free in my heart—always.

The Deck Ducks

The baby season of 1993 was definitely a winner in terms of "cuteness" and volume. We raised dozens of orphaned little teddy bear–shaped raccoons, dear little coyote pups, bob kittens, Cooper's hawks, barn owls, just to name a few of the cutest. Not much, however, could compare with our sixteen baby mallards. These little green-and-yellow "fluffs" arrived courtesy of our San Diego County Department of Animal Control.

The friendly Animal Control officers in our area are perhaps the most concerned and caring folks we know. Dealing with irresponsible pet owners and stray or injured dogs and cats is a tough job, yet each year these officers cheerfully bring literally hundreds of orphaned or injured wild mammals and birds to us for care. This is not actually part of their job description, but they willingly do so because of their concern for the wildlife.

Three different animal-control officers drove up our driveway one week, each bearing a handful of tiny day-old mallards. By the end of the week we had our sixteen. Although we raised many more than sixteen that spring, this first little group was special.

They stayed in our medical facility for several months, under heat lamps and with strict dietary supervision. Baby ducks are able to feed themselves immediately after birth, much to Michelle's dismay. She would rather hand-feed or bottle-feed an orphan than anything else in the world. With the mallards, she only had to present a dish of their favorite foods: ground scratch, bird seed, grasses, tubifex worms and their all-time favorite—Science Diet cat food. These babies did beautifully and quickly outgrew the medical center.

In late spring we moved them to "The Ritz," an outdoor enclosure. They still had their heat lamp but also had tall green grass and a swimming pool. In the daytime, they would

swim and forage in the grass. At night, these sixteen little babies with no mother would huddle together under the lamp, forming a tight little group, each one reliant on the other for warmth and companionship.

As the evenings got warmer and they began developing pinfeathers, they needed the heat lamp less and less, until finally we were able to remove it completely. They still slept as a tightly knit, bonded little bunch. They began developing their semi-adult feathers, and it was time to move them to a larger enclosure, one in which they could spread their wings and develop some flying skills.

The logical choice was to put them in our large protected "fowl yard." This is home to our pet chickens, turkeys, geese

Because They Matter

and domestic ducks. It is shaded by beautiful honey locust and eucalyptus trees, with many shelters and a great "pond" made from an old fiberglass TV satellite dish.

Michelle, Chuck and I were so excited the day we moved them, since it would give them a wonderful opportunity to begin flying practice. Apparently the "wicked sixteen" had other ideas. We had no sooner moved them all to their new home when they said "no, thanks, we're outta here." (I suspect that Mother, our overbearing goose, had something to do with this mass exodus.)

Anyway, for about eight hours we had juvenile mallards wandering all over our five acres. Attempts to capture them were useless, so we just hoped for the best. At almost sunset that summer evening, we heard a resounding "quack, quack, quack, quack," and ducks began rushing from everywhere. (Rushing for a juvenile duck means waddling really fast!)

This "mad quacker" had apparently located a safe spot for settling in and wanted her friends to know about it. She had chosen a spot that is off limits to visitors, an area in which we keep large tubs of water for any of our visiting wildlife. Overhead is a canopy of shade trees that keeps the area cool, moist and protected. Science Diet cat food is also provided in this area for crows, ravens, squirrels and assorted nocturnal visitors. This became the sanctuary for our little mallards.

During the daylight hours this little group could be seen waddling all over the property, stopping periodically for a rest or a swim or a dabble or to occasionally eat a lovely vinca, azalea or geranium. This latter vice did not sit well with the staff members who had carefully nurtured these plants, but there wasn't much anyone could do. Besides, they *were* really cute while they were eating the flowers.

Every evening at sunset, from out of nowhere, we would hear "quack, quack, quack, quack"—always a series of four quacks, each quack quieter than the preceding one. The little troops would come marching home to their designated sanctuary and settle in together for the evening—all sixteen. (Chuck and I counted them every night.)

After several weeks of this, we finally located the "chief quacker." It was a little female mallard, the same age as all the others, who had apparently named herself as the guardian of her little friends. They listened to her, too. When she quacked, they came!

As they got a little older, they began trying to fly. Chuck and I were so honored to be able to watch the first duckling take its first flight. He ran across the yard, furiously flapping his wings, and after about thirty feet of running, liftoff occurred. He flew only about five feet before landing occurred. Landing was not nearly as pretty as liftoff, however. He skidded on his bottom, overcorrected this error and went beak first into the dirt.

Chuck and I nevertheless applauded his efforts, since we did not want him to feel like a failure. We needn't have done so. After he regained his composure and joined his fifteen friends, he was greeted as if he had won the Nobel Peace Prize.

Fifteen little ducks rushed to his side—quack, quack, quacking and nibbling his beak. What a hero! For the next few weeks, more and more of the ducklings accomplished this

Because They Matter

marvelous feat and were equally welcomed by their comrades upon landing.

Pretty soon they were soaring around the property and really looking grand. By this time, all but six of them were flying. One of the six was Guardian Duckling. Apparently she saw no need to fly, as she still had five ducklings on the ground to care for.

Before I move on, I have to get this off my chest: I do not believe that ducks are aerodynamically correct, and I cannot figure out for the life of me how they can fly. They have these enormously chubby bodies, and to take off, their wings must do 5,000 rpm just to get two feet off the ground. They look like enormous hummingbirds, flapping their wings faster than the speed of light just to get a two-foot lift! Well, fly they do, and quite well, although I do not yet know how. Landings are an equal mystery.

Although I suppose they land on water quite well, I have never seen a graceful ground landing. The landings are either butt first or beak first, never feet first. They always tumble, yet quickly regain their poise (such as it is with a duck).

Personally, if I had to fly and it required that much effort to get off the ground, and if I knew that when I wanted to come back to earth I would either have to scrape my rump or land on my head, darned if I wouldn't try to find another mode of transportation!

By spring of 1993 the deck on our house desperately needed to be restained. It had been two years since it had last been done, and it had really weathered. Longtime staffer Peter Krutz and I decided to wait until we had a lull in baby season to undertake this project. We had hundreds of babies in the medical center, and Chuck was extremely busy with construction of our huge new flight cage (along with a thousand other things he had to do). So Peter and I decided that this would be our project. I would supervise and boost Peter's teenage male ego, and he would stain.

By summer the lull hit and we were ready to stain except for one little hitch: We had six ducks living on our deck that we did not dare disturb! Deck staining would have to wait.

To backtrack a little, ten of our ducklings finally became completely adept (for ducks) at flying; five were still too young, and Guardian Duck had to care for these five. The ten "flyers" would stay away all day long, yet each afternoon at almost sunset, Guardian Duck would take her position on our concrete wall and quack her charges home.

She would do her four quacks, and seconds later a horde of ducks would fly overhead, make successive passes and divide into small groups. Eventually all would land, either on their rear ends or heads, but they would land and settle in for an hour or so.

The ten would eventually leave before nightfall to places unknown, leaving Guardian and her troops alone.

Guardian apparently decided to seek out greener pastures but did not want to go too far. Since Science Diet is also served on the deck in the evening for Blaine and Annie the turkeys, Sweet Pea and Pompous the peacocks, and for any stragglers (stray cats, toads, slugs or anyone else who might need a square meal), Guardian decided the deck was the place to be. Just at sunset, she and her five peer babies would waddle down the driveway to the deck, nibble on some cat food and curl up on our doorstep for the evening.

Chuck and I felt good that they knew they were safe on our doorstep, so we never made any effort to deter them—in fact we enjoyed it. If we had to rush out in the middle of the night on an emergency, the deck ducks would quietly quack in protest but move to let us out the front door and then quickly return to the doormat when we were gone.

The only problem with this was the impossibility of staining the deck as long as the deck ducks remained. Ducks defecate all the time. Our deck had a crusty white coating that would require many hours of scrubbing prior to staining, and I was beginning to wonder if we would ever be able to take care of it. We pride ourselves on keeping our facility well maintained, and our deck was becoming an embarrassment.

By late August our deck-duck population was at four, as two of Guardian's charges had taken flight with the others. Diligent little Guardian continued her late-afternoon ritual of quacking her wayward ones home. She would stand on the wall, do her quacks and wait for their landing. We became fascinated with this daily ritual for two reasons: It always occurred when the sinking sun hit a precise spot on her wall; and there were now forty ducks landing every afternoon, not just her little thirteen or fourteen juveniles, but beautiful green-headed adult males and large, lovely adult females.

Guardian was inviting the whole world over for afternoon tea! Every evening they would all quack, dabble and mingle for awhile and then in small groups fly away again after about an hour, leaving Guardian and her dwindling number to themselves. This little group would then quietly quack themselves down to the deck, eat a little and go to bed.

For several weeks in August and September, friends and neighbors would stop by just to watch our "quacking ceremony," when forty ducks were called in and came every afternoon with butt and beak landings all over the place.

In late August, Chuck and I gave a party for our staff and volunteers. We were a little concerned about Guardian and friends that evening, as the party was to be held on our (still-unstained) deck. We need not have worried, as Guardian followed her evening ritual, disregarding the thirty people standing on "her bed." She and her friends stood on the edge of the deck and quacked incessantly at the thirty intruders. After about ten minutes of this, our guests sheepishly came in the house. Guardian took her position on the doormat, and we continued our party—indoors.

By the end of September, Guardian was alone—all of her "babies" had flown away. She spent her days in solitude, swimming in the tubs we provided, dabbling and napping. She would quack her forty-plus friends home every evening and greet them warmly. They would leave, and she would make her way down to her doormat for the night.

Our hearts were breaking for this lovely, nurturing little duck who had taken it upon herself to care for and "mother" her fellow orphans. We found nothing physically wrong with Guardian; there didn't seem to be any reason for her not flying and joining the others.

After several days of watching her lonely routine, we decided to try something. Our lovely fowl yard, home to our

Because They Matter

assortment of domestic chickens, geese and turkeys, had recently become home to three permanently disabled (nonflying) juvenile mallards. Two of them had been shot and one was hit by a car, leaving each of them with an irreparably damaged wing. They are permanent residents and seem quite content; they have companionship, a "swimmin' hole," great food and protection.

One Sunday afternoon in early October, Peter and I netted Guardian and put her in the yard. She quickly found the juveniles, quacked and nibbled their beaks and has never made any attempt to leave them. She seems happy and can be seen nearly every afternoon either bathing or snoozing or dabbling with three little crippled ducks always by her side.

For several afternoons after we put her in the yard, a huge group of ducks would fly and circle overhead but never land. They were waiting for Guardian to quack them home, but she was busy with her new babies. We have never seen them again.

Our concern will always be with this lovely group of forty-plus mallards who trusted us and trusted Guardian to quack them "home." Even if only for a short while, they knew they were safe from hunters' bullets and all of the other evils provided courtesy of "mankind."

If there were ever a "Mother of the Year" award in the wildlife kingdom, little Guardian should be the recipient. Although well under a year old, this little duck took it upon herself to protect her peers from harm for as long as she could, until their own wild instincts became an overpowering force. She has chosen to stay and will probably be a wonderful surrogate mother to future little orphaned mallards who come to us.

Our deck has now been scrubbed and restained and looks lovely. I must admit, though, we do miss that white crusty coating that let us know that "for humans, you are not too bad" in the duck world.

Brave

This turkey vulture is not, nor has she ever been, a client of ours, although I think she'd like to be and has tried on several occasions to become one. We're pretty sure her story started several years ago, the summer when all the vultures came.

Almost overnight we had become home base to about thirty vultures. As our knowledge about vultures grew, we realized that much of what we were seeing were family units, most probably patient mothers and their fledgling offspring. Brave Vulture, we surmised, was one of that first group of juveniles to visit us with their mothers.

As the years have passed, she has made this her permanent home and rarely leaves. You might ask yourself at this point, "How does this woman know one turkey vulture from another?" My response is that by simply observing them, one notices differences either in behavior or appearance. Brave has a little row of what I would call warts (she would, of course, call them beauty marks) across her brow. Chuck and I and all our staff can recognize her in a flash. She became very obvious to us on several occasions.

One such incident we refer to as "the mystery of the extra vulture." At that time we had three vultures in residence in our large flight cage. One Sunday morning, volunteer and bird watcher extraordinaire Stan Brown asked us about the fourth vulture in the flight cage. We assured Stan that we had only the three regulars, as no more had come into our center. Stan was adamant that there were four and did a second head count.

There truly were four vultures in the enclosure. In all her shining glory, there stood Brave acting as if she belonged there. After a quick search we found a hole at the very top of the flight cage. Our neighborhood vultures and ravens had been spotted toying with something up there, and it was only then that we realized that it was the thread that we had used to sew the flight cage netting together that they had found so amusing.

Although none of the rehab birds had checked out of our hotel, at least one "outsider" had checked herself in. We allowed Brave a few days of R&R in the enclosure, since she seemed so content, before setting her free. I think we were all kind of proud that an outside bird had found our enclosure so inviting that she wanted to be on the inside looking out rather than just the opposite.

We repaired the hole, yet Brave was not deterred. She apparently made a friend while in the "slammer," and we would watch her for days on end, standing on the ground outside the large flight cage accepting bits of blades of grass or bits of food from one of the vultures inside the enclosure. That particular flight cage had wooden slats, spaced about an inch apart at its base, and it was through these slats that these gifts were given.

Brave reciprocated these gifts by passing similar morsels to the one inside. To this day, this practice still continues between Brave and the vulture in the flight cage (a permanent resident, due to his disability). We don't know what it means, but it certainly means something to Brave and her captive friend.

Because They Matter

Late summer of 1994 brought another twist to Brave's story. At that time, she began being very brave indeed and would stand on the wall outside our office and peer at us through the window with the most "pleading vulture look" she could muster. She wanted some food—*then!* She obviously did not mean to wait till late afternoon when Chuck passed out food to our "clients" in the flight cages and to all the

neighborhood transients. We would put food out for her, as she ordered, at which time she would fly a short distance away, wait for us to leave, then return to eat.

On one of those days when she returned, she arrived with company—a fledgling vulture. We'll never know for sure whether this baby was Brave's offspring or just a youngster who happened to know a good thing when he saw it. They returned together on several occasions that summer and fall, and then Brave Baby, probably not as impatient as Brave One, blended in with the usual vulture crowd.

Starting with the Deck Ducks, the lovely redwood deck attached to the front of our home has become the haven for many creatures. It has, in fact, become so popular that Chuck and I are unable to use it at all. Our patio furniture has long since been relocated to an area so far undiscovered by these "homesteaders." To enter the front door of our home to eat or to go to bed after a long day, we must perform an entire sequence of apologies to those we have disturbed.

Our nightly routine consists of "I'm sorry, Blaine and Annie (the turkeys)"; "Excuse us, Pompous, Sweet Pea, Tweedledumb and Tweedledumber (the peacocks and peahens)"; "It's okay, Crow and Wak-Waa." "Good night, Baby, good night, Booger (the cats)."

There are no apologies given to the many frogs and slugs, as I'm not sure they understand, but we are very careful not to disturb them while they sleep, eat and generally do frog and slug "things." Our most recent apology has become "It's okay, Brave, you don't have to fly away." While Brave is not a regular on the deck like everyone else, she's there once in a while, and I am always singularly touched by her presence.

The first time she came to our deck is still a fond memory. It was early October, and we had had a cold snap. (A cold snap in our neck of the woods is sixty-nine degrees, and we pull out our winter parkas.)

This hideous frigid weather was followed by a torrential downpour that none of us, humans or nonhumans, were prepared for. We got about a hundredth of an inch of rain in three or four hours. Some would call this a sprinkle, but we are in a drought in Southern California, and this was *rain!* Chuck and I had let our staff leave early, as all the necessary work had been done, and we don't get too many emergency calls during bad weather. It seems that most people and animals tend to find their havens and ride out "the storm."

It was late afternoon, and I had been catching up on a backlog of paperwork, reading, correspondence, and a lengthy play period with our seventeen house cats (this is Cleveland Amory's fault), when I stopped just to watch the gentle rain and relax a bit.

There she was on the railing, this dear, sweet vulture who had come to trust us. Our frogs were "singin' in the rain" and hopping around, our four goofy peacocks were all hunkered down on the deck railing, and right in the middle of them, with her lovely red head tucked away in contentment, was Brave Vulture.

I stood at the door, not five feet away from her as she slept, and marveled not only at her exterior beauty, but also the trusting, kind spirit within her that has allowed all of us here the special opportunity to observe and study the wonders, the antics and the gracious behavior of the turkey vulture.

Path

Path came to us in the spring of 1993.

She was about six days old, weighed almost a pound and looked remarkably like a Chihuahua puppy. The coyote ears I love so much had not yet become coyote ears; instead they were little brown flaps pasted to the side of her head. The lovely coyote muzzle and the coyote grin had not yet happened either. Path had a little flat face, and we all speculated that maybe she wasn't a coyote after all! She surely didn't look like one then.

Our concerns were soon allayed in the way she took to the bottle. Even at that early age, coyotes have that marvelous will to live. With many newly orphaned animals, getting them to suckle from a nipple that isn't mama's can be a nightmare.

Path had no problem—food was food. Because she was so young, her chances of becoming imprinted on humans (despite our efforts to the opposite) were pretty strong, especially since we didn't have coyote pups her age to commingle with her. Orphaned coyote pups usually come in batches rather than alone. Path's situation was a little odd, and I've often wondered what became of her siblings.

That April our medical center was filled with orphans of almost every wild species found in California: baby birds, possums, skunks, raccoons and more. Our staff members (who spend a minimum of eight hours a day putting food in some little orphan's mouth and loving every minute of it) concluded that because Path was with no other pups, one person should be responsible for her care in hopes that if she did imprint, it would be on only one person.

I solemnly agreed and volunteered for this most "hideous" task. Even though I knew that staffers Michelle Lyons and Sharon Casey frequently ogled her, and I saw evidence that her bedding had been changed or rearranged when I wasn't around, Path was *mine*.

Path was almost weaned at three weeks. She would eat anything put in front of her. She loved ground chicken mixed with her formula, and squished grapes. She thrived and soon became mature enough to join the older coyote pups. We had two others in the medical center at that time. They were weaned and had a huge, sunny room to themselves.

We introduced Path to these two, and she was thrilled. I still remember peeking through the recovery-room door and watching her run from one pup to the other, grinning, rolling over in submission and becoming a coyote. By this time, Path looked like a coyote—mostly. Her little ear flaps now stood at attention, her muzzle was becoming elongated, and her little baby-blue eyes were getting a golden tint to them. She did love her coyote pals and became one of them, but she loved me, too.

Cleaning up their room was a true adventure. Coyotes go to the bathroom a lot, especially well-fed pups. I am convinced that they also have evening parties, wherein they dance in their poop and attempt to paint the walls with it as well.

The recovery room that housed these three pups has heavy-duty vinyl flooring and walls to allow for easier clean-up and disinfecting. Mornings would find the floors and walls

Because They Matter

truly a work of brown art. Mornings would also find Path eager to see a human being with food—so eager that she would jump on the designated human to get the food. I often left that room with Path's little works of art smeared all over my clothes.

Needless to say, we were thrilled when Path and friends were big enough to join the older coyote pups in an outdoor enclosure. Adding Path and her two friends to this large enclosure gave us a total of thirteen pups outside.

Well, Path was in her glory. It was her duty to jump on and befriend every pup, and she worked at this for hours every day. She loved them all and was so truly happy to be among them. There are lone coyotes and there are pack coyotes. Path was a pack coyote and tried desperately to make her new friends the same. She was an absolute joy to watch, as she was always busy. Late afternoons, right before the evening feeding, she became her most joyful self—bouncing in the air, running up logs, chasing errant mockingbirds, grinning, tussling and wagging that coyote tail. We get great joy from watching coyote pups play—and play they do!

The orphans who come to us are cared for and well protected, consequently they are apparently unaware of the dangers that lie ahead for them. I continued to be the sole food provider in the evenings, and Path continued to be thrilled to see me. I would stomp my feet and make scary noises that would send twelve pups running for cover, while one—Path, of course—would crouch, grin and roll over. I was concerned as I didn't want her to like humans. I could not explain to her that she could trust me and no one else.

As the days went by and I continued making my scary noises, Path became a little more skittish and more reliant on her coyote friends. This made me feel better. To me, a wildlife rehabber's failing marks are in the number of animals permanently tamed or imprinted by that person. It's unethical, dangerous and unfair to the wildlife.

Early one Saturday evening when I went in to feed the pups, something nudged my leg. I looked down and Path was resting her little coyote head on my leg and looking at me. She was sick. I grabbed her and called for Chuck; we took her to the medical center where her life with us had begun. She was slightly dehydrated, so we gave her some IV fluids and set a regimen for the next day as well.

She was a wonderful patient and accepted her fluids and antibiotic injections without complaining. She didn't eat Sunday night, so Michelle, Sharon and I continued her fluids and antibiotics on Monday and attempted to feed her small bits of food.

She rallied a bit on Tuesday and ate a little food. She had regressed to the "baby Path," so we held her, which she loved. As long as she was being held, we were able to administer fluids and do other necessary procedures without a problem.

Because They Matter

She seemed better so we were optimistic. No longer worried about taming or imprinting at this point, we were concerned with keeping Path alive.

If I could have kept her alive by kissing her little pointy nose and ears all night long, I would have. I kissed her good-night that evening after her medication. She seemed comfortable and content. Wednesday morning she was gone. My heart was truly broken, but showing emotion in a job such as ours is a no-no. We have our losses, and we all must deal with them in our own individual way, but privately.

I buried Path, cried quietly to myself, not just for her, but for me and for the sad plight of all coyotes. I covered her little grave with wild mustard blossoms. I loved that little scamp, and I will forever miss her.

To truly know and love a coyote is a very special thing, and I knew her as well as she knew me. My skinny face was the first thing she saw when she opened her little blue eyes at fourteen days of age. Mine was also the last face she saw with her golden eyes at ten weeks of age.

Many wild animals, upon sensing imminent death, will retreat to a dark, quiet area to pass away. In the case of wild animals in our care, those who die are generally found in the back of the carrier or enclosure in which they are kept. Path's little body was at the front of her enclosure. I will always believe that she passed away while looking for me. I wish I had been there for her.

Her name, Path, came from Melinda Worth Popham's book *Skywater*, in which a mother coyote, at her moment of dying, nuzzled her pup and uttered:

"Path, little moon-caller,
may you live a completed path."

My Path's path was not very long but was certainly completed. She brought to me and others who knew her a world of joy and an insight into coyote puppyhood that few have ever seen.

"The Thing"

We get calls—boy do we ever get calls.

While we deal only with the ill, injured or orphaned native wildlife of Southern California, we answer calls regarding parrots, ocelots, black panthers, ferrets, alligators and goodness knows what else people see (or think they see) in their pristine suburban neighborhoods.

Our last suburban mountain lion call turned out to be a friendly golden retriever. Most of the time we can handle these odd calls without responding. They generally turn out to be free-roaming dogs, large domestic cats, oversized lizards and sometimes things that just can't be explained but are never seen again.

None of the above was the case on a call we received one Sunday afternoon. An elderly woman in an area about fifteen miles from us called shortly before sunset to report a large, shiny black animal with tentacles that had been threatening her since early that morning. The animal was in her backyard and periodically would raise its head and flash its tentacles as if ready to attack.

The woman was absolutely horrified, and her description of the animal sounded like nothing we had ever heard of. We asked her if a neighbor might be able to identify the animal and help determine whether it was ill or injured. We were not looking forward to a wild goose chase at that time of day when we still had several hours of evening feedings to do.

After a couple of phone calls back and forth, we learned

that she did not know her neighbors, her husband was in the hospital, and the creature was still in her yard bobbing and waving its arms. It was getting closer to dark, she was very frightened, and Chuck was too curious to ignore this one.

We gathered a carrier, catch pole, flashlight and some other gear and headed out. It was almost dark when we arrived. She was standing just inside her closed screen door. She tersely pointed to the side-gate entrance to her backyard. She stayed in the house but stood at a rear window, which she had cracked about an inch to help us locate "the thing."

Chuck and I quietly approached the edge of the patio where the creature was purported to be. We began shining our flashlights and spotted the hideous monster in all its gleaming and gesticulating glory.

Chuck and I exhaled deeply, as this had been a tense time for all of us. "The thing" was a torn piece of a black plastic trash bag. The waving motions had been caused by the gentle breeze blowing that summer day.

Chuck picked up the "creature," held it about fifteen feet from the lady at the window and asked, "Is this what you saw, ma'am?" The old lady grabbed her chest, reeled a few steps

Because They Matter

away from the window and mouthed (as I guess she couldn't speak at that particular time) "Yes." Chuck let her know that it was just a bit of trash and not to worry, nothing would harm her. Her ensuing actions then had us mesmerized. She slammed the rear window shut and closed the curtains, without uttering a word. We let ourselves out the side gate and proceeded toward the front. As we walked those few steps, we heard the front door slam shut. I guess she didn't want one of our business cards.

Chuck and I, with "the thing" curled up in my hand, jumped in the car and exploded in laughter. This escapade had put us way behind schedule but had been a great tension reliever. I set up "the thing" in the medical center when we returned and put a DO NOT TOUCH sign on the cage. We got another couple of hours of laughs the next day when we related the story to our staff.

I cannot explain the rudeness of the woman we helped that afternoon. She had had a rough day, I'll give her that. We had helped her out, expecting and certainly getting nothing in return. A "thank you" would have been sufficient. Later that night, after her exhibition of disdain for us had set in, I secretly hoped that "the thing" would crawl in her bed that night and wave his shiny head right in her old cranky face.

Sumo

Newborn tree squirrels look like little monkey embryos (or what we would imagine monkey embryos to look like). These helpless little babies do not even resemble their flamboyant, graceful adult counterparts.

Sumo and his weak little brother were the first and only baby tree squirrels we dealt with in the spring of 1993. These babies were accidentally taken from their nest and away from their mother by an acquaintance of ours who happens to be a tree trimmer. Tom had been contracted by an individual to trim some limbs from a tree on his property. While trimming, Tom inadvertently trimmed a branch holding the squirrel nest. Branch, nest and babies hit the ground before Tom even realized the nest was there and could do anything.

Fortunately, Tom brought the babies to us. As is so often the case in the spring and summer, many animals' nests are destroyed by people who are just not thinking. Tree trimming should not be done when animals are nesting. Fall and winter months are by far the safest times (for the wildlife).

We prepared special formula for our two newest babies and got them warm. Even during the heat of the summer, baby animals chill rapidly, as they cannot yet regulate their own body temperature. Consequently, we keep most of our youngsters on heating pads.

After warming them and stimulating them to go to the bathroom, the babies were hungry and squirming. So with our syringes full of formula and rigged with nipples for squirrels, we fed them the first of many feedings to come. For the first few days, we fed them every three hours around the clock, then gradually eliminated the two middle-of-the-night feedings.

Sumo thrived. His little brother was very weak and had some internal bleeding from the fall. He lived only about ten days. As is often the case, none of our fellow rehabbers had baby tree squirrels, so Sumo was raised alone. His development seemed so slow to us, partly due to the fact that we were anxious for him to mature.

One of our staff members continued to insist that he was a monkey, so we were eagerly waiting for some tree-squirrel traits to appear. During his feedings, this bald, blind, palm-sized little "whatever" wriggled in our hands like a snake until he connected with his "titty" at which time he eagerly consumed his special diet. The name Sumo came about because he so resembled a Sumo wrestler. He was a thick, muscular little critter and, after feeding, his little belly became firm and round like that of the Japanese wrestler.

Sumo's eyes finally opened, and from day one they had a wicked, wary little glint to them. He was getting some hair and beginning to look like a squirrel. Our next concern became his tail. His tail at this stage of his development was a hairy little appendage that just followed him around. Adult tree squirrels have flashy, bushy tails that seem to have a mind of their own.

Sumo grew and grew—belly first, of course—and still "the tail" was like an eager servant following close behind its master. We became concerned that he had a defective tail. All

Because They Matter

of us, as rehabbers and animal lovers in general, often worry about the strangest things. In Sumo's case, a defective tail would be a real problem for survival, as the tail is helpful for maintaining balance and for attracting girl squirrels.

Sumo soon became old enough to graduate from his nest to a cage equipped not with "monkey bars" but "squirrel bars" —his own set. We knew now that he really was a squirrel. We eased up on his feedings, began introducing more natural squirrel foods, and Sumo, instead of sleeping most of the day, could be seen cavorting on his gym set during the daylight hours.

His tail did devel-op normally, which we quickly discovered one morning when staffer Sandy Casey opened his cage to begin clean-up. With no warning, Sumo leapt out of his cage onto Sandy's head. His beady little eyes  were darting back and forth, and his just-furred little tail was bushed out and curled over his back. He had not needed to exercise his tail until that moment. This incident let us know that it was time for bigger and better things for Sumo. He was completely weaned and eating all-natural tree squirrel foods.

We moved him to a large outdoor enclosure equipped with branches and logs and began to minimize our contact with him. He was, nonetheless, imprinted on us and not afraid of humans. Releasing him was going to be difficult. This strong, healthy little squirrel needed his freedom, yet he needed to be watched to make sure that he developed normal relationships with other squirrels and could function in the wild as a real tree squirrel should.

Dorothy Mushet, our friend and fellow tree-squirrel aficionado, offered to "hack" Sumo out on her property. This was a triple blessing for us, since Sumo originally came from an area very near Dorothy's house; she had many tree squirrels on her property already; and her daughter, Cindy Mushet-Rogers, is also a wildlife rehabber should Sumo need some assistance while adjusting to the outdoors.

Cindy and Dorothy put Sumo—cage and all—under their oak trees. Sumo was to stay caged for several days to acclimate himself to the neighborhood and to the sight and smell of the other squirrels.

One lovely summer day, Dorothy left Sumo's cage door open, yet continued to put food in his cage. Sumo nervously stepped out and raced up the nearest tree. This brave little youngster was about to discover a whole new world. He played in the oaks all day long and cavorted with other squirrels. At sundown on this first night and for several nights afterward, Sumo returned to his cage to sleep. Old habits are hard to break. Eventually Sumo did not return to the cage but stayed with his newfound squirrel friends.

Sumo finally became a truly wild squirrel and made only one faux pas in the early stages of "wilding up." One afternoon, Dorothy's husband, Buzz, happened to be standing under Sumo's favorite tree. Apparently forgetting himself for a moment and obviously thrilled at the presence of a former friend, Sumo leapt off his branch onto Buzz's back. Realizing what he had done, Sumo scampered up Buzz's shoulders and quickly raced back to his oak tree, where he glared nervously at the human tree.

Sumo rarely leaves his lovely oak trees now except to be the first squirrel at the dish of snacks Dorothy occasionally puts out for him and his pals. Our hope for Sumo is that he will always stay where he is now. This is one of the reasons Dorothy continues to provide snacks for him.

So many other people view these lovely creatures as objects that must be destroyed. They are routinely shot, trapped and poisoned by individuals who fail to see the beauty, the spirit or the value of these joyful little animals.

Eggward, the Party Balloons and the Last Straw

Eggward came to us in a rather unconventional manner in the summer of 1993. He arrived in a dilapidated station wagon and was unceremoniously handed to us by an elderly lady wearing a T-shirt covered in raven poop. As she handed him over, she smiled and said, "I stole this bird from my neighbor, and I knew you'd take good care of him." I liked her immediately and thanked her for saving the raven's life.

Her neighbor had apparently found a young raven and had raised him on a diet of scrambled eggs. So in addition to being very tame and imprinted on humans, Eggward was suffering from malnutrition. He had received plenty of food, just not enough variation. His condition was similar to our eating nothing but apples day after day—getting full but at the same time not receiving proper nutrition.

We set up Eggward in the medical center and fed him a huge variety of food, which he savored! Within a couple of weeks, he looked "mahvelous." His feathers were purple-black and glossy, and his mouth color was a healthy deep pink. We got to know his mouth very well as it was always open. Although Eggward was beyond the "gaping stage" that most baby birds go through until they are able to feed themselves, he continued to "gape" through adolescence because of his reliance on humans.

Improperly raised wild birds tend to be somewhat retarded in their development and do "baby behaviors" well into adulthood. There is hardly anything cuter than a nest of baby ravens at feeding time, I must admit. They are so happy to see the "food person" coming that they all attempt to stand on their barely developed legs, flap their scraggly little pinfeather wings and open their rosy-pink mouths as wide as they will open, hoping for any little morsel to slide down their throats.

I am always reminded of a vase of tulips each time I see a nest of baby ravens at feeding time. Well, poor little teenage Eggward did these behaviors and looked so silly. He would even sleep with his mouth agape, just in case some "food person" came along at nap time. He was cute but dumb.

A favorite movie of ours is *Edward Scissorhands*. So assuming we would have this raven for a while, we decided to name him Eggward Peckerhead, a play on the movie title and a remembrance of his former diet of scrambled eggs.

Physically, Eggward flourished; mentally was a different story. He spent weeks in an outdoor flight cage with other ravens and, being a nice raven, enjoyed the companionship of his own kind. However, if a human approached, he became Mr. Tulip-mouth, gaping at anybody!

The enormous enjoyment we derive from these little wild creatures who come to love us so much is tempered by the fact that their survival rate in the wild is severely diminished because of their reliance on and fondness for humans. We simply do the best we can to reduce their affinity for us and to make them self-sufficient.

The day finally arrived for Eggward to learn to be a wild raven. We released him from his enclosure with great trepidation. He was obviously thrilled and played raven games to his heart's content. We became "guardedly optimistic" (an ominous term) as he traveled into ravenhood. We knew he would be fine as long as he stayed nearby.

As luck would have it, Eggward disappeared one morning while we were busy with our daily chores. We were too busy to notice his absence until we received the first of many phone calls to come. Eggward had apparently sauntered into a neighbor's yard and was making a fool of himself—talking, gaping and acting like a lost child. He was enjoying the grapes he was being fed, so he wasn't too distraught.

Michelle Lyons and staffer Rick Over rushed over to re-trieve Eggward. They had to explain to the neighbor all of the reasons why wild animals don't make good pets, as the neigh-bors had really wanted to put him in a cage. After hearing all about Eggward's situation and what we were trying to do, the neighbors completely understood.

We jailed Eggward again and released him after a few weeks. Eggward the rambler immediately took another road trip after a few days and wound up with the same neighbor, who again promptly called us. This cycle continued for a cou-ple of months: Incarcerate Eggward, release Eggward, pick up Eggward at the neighbor's house (thank God for an under-standing neighbor). We finally learned his routine: When we bored him or became too busy to toss him snacks, he booked.

The last straw finally came when our neighbor called (for the umpteenth time) to inform us of Eggward's whereabouts. This time, however, was a little more serious. He had appar-ently been somewhere else first and had wound up getting himself wound up in a bunch of party balloons. There he was in Pat's yard—strutting, gaping and talking, with a group of multicolored balloons hanging brightly over his head. A real easy mark for someone who doesn't understand ravens.

Rick volunteered to fetch Eggward one more time. When Rick got to Pat's, Eggward had already vacated the premises. Rick made a thorough search and found nothing. A dejected Rick returned to the center to prepare us for an all-out raven hunt.

To his extreme pleasure, he was greeted in the driveway by a silly little raven wearing a halo of balloons. We were all relieved, yet at the same time we realized that "next time" for Eggward could result in tragedy.

We all put our heads together and came up with the perfect solution: Pawn Eggward off to a responsible, caring person who knew ravens, had lots of property and could keep an eye on our little misfit. Our friend and fellow rehabber Cindy Mushet-Rogers fit that description perfectly. She consented to take Eggward, incarcerate him for a couple of weeks, let him go and hope for the best.

Well, for several days after his parole at Cindy's, Eggward was just Eggward. He charmed everyone, including Cindy's husband, Blake, who somehow acquired a strange little black appendage at his heel when he did his morning and evening chores on their ranch. (It could have had something to do with the grapes that Blake kept in his pocket and freely passed out to any raven who might be hanging around.)

Cindy later reported that Eggward had been seen cavorting with other ravens who live on their property. This was very encouraging.

Because They Matter

Chuck and I speculated on whether "The Egg" would return here. We assumed he wouldn't because the thirty-five-mile trip involves some desolate terrain, and ravens tend to congregate close to people. Well, we were wrong! Late one afternoon, we spotted a young raven on the back of our property. I was able to get within five feet of him before he casually hopped away.

Eggward was back, but this time with several raven friends. I could tell he was much too embarrassed to do silly "Eggward things" in front of his friends, so I did not push the issue. I left and re-turned with a nice dish of raven snacks. I called to Eggward (who turned his head away from me like a petulant child) and put the dish under  the dead eucalyptus tree where Eggward and his twenty friends were perched. As I walked away, I whispered, "Good-bye, Eggward, have a good life."

My melodramatic whisper to "The Egg" was a little pre-mature, however, as he continues to be with us to this day. He is much wiser now and knows raven ways, but he will always be Eggward to us.

He comes and goes at will and knows, as other ravens do, that this is home. Just like a kid off to college, he comes home when he's hungry or tired of the day-to-day hassles that life can bring. We are his haven, and as his self-confidence grows, he will need us less and less. We will then, with great joy and deep sadness, really say "Goodbye Eggward" for the last time.

Dog Bite

Possums (opossums) are not necessarily the "cutest" of all the wildlife we deal with here, but they are certainly the most fascinating. They are the only North American marsupial, they have a life span of less than five years and have more teeth than any other North American animal.

While they all look basically alike, possums have distinct and often charming personalities. Some are large and aggressive when threatened, while others are kind of slow-moving and pretty peaceable little critters.

We deal with hundreds on an annual basis, yet none so typifies the courage and spunk of these often-ignored, sometimes-vilified, lovely animals as Dog Bite, a young juvenile who had been severely mauled by a dog. To compound her problems, her injuries were several days old and massively infected. Kind people had seen her tangle with a dog but had been unable to catch her until her injuries had caused her near demise.

A fracture at the shoulder of her left front leg was the least of her problems. There were puncture wounds, hideous signs of infection, and maggots completely surrounding her neck area. The skin had been torn to the point that bones and tendons were exposed. We quickly cleaned her wounds, removed the maggots, administered IV fluids, treated her for shock and gave her a healthy dose of antibiotics.

One of the major problems in dealing with injured wildlife is the stress they experience from human contact. It is imperative that we work quickly and silently and immediately place the animal in a warm, quiet place to alleviate this stress factor.

We cleaned her up as best we could that day, knowing we had several days of cleaning ahead of us before we could truly assess the damage. We weren't sure she would even survive that first night, but we provided her with plenty of food and fresh water, just in case. In many such "iffy" cases, we'll work with an animal for several days, looking for any glimmer of improvement or any sign of a will to live on the animal's part. Nonhuman animals suffer pain so stoically and have such remarkable recuperative powers that in many cases we let the animal be the judge of his or her own fate.

Well, Dog Bite sealed her own fate on her first night with us that spring. Michelle had prepared chopped grapes, chopped chicken and canned cat food for Dog Bite's first meal with us. By morning, she had consumed everything! She had to be in enormous pain from her injuries, yet she showed us that she really wanted to live.

We knew it would be a long road for her, but we were determined to offer our support. Other than just supplying food to keep her alive, we had to clean her wounds every day and administer oral antibiotics twice a day.

Because it is nearly impossible to pin a fracture in a possum's leg, that injury was going to have to heal on its own. Our job would be to limit her exercise and let nature do the rest. The huge wounds around her neck remained open for weeks; suturing was out of the question—there was no skin to suture.

Because They Matter

Every morning we pulled her out for cleaning and disinfecting. She never fought us, although this must have been an extremely painful ordeal. After about three weeks of this regimen, we realized that there was no longer the stench associated with a massive infection. We also observed tiny bits of actual healing taking place. This little fighter was going to make it!

Dog Bite stayed in our medical center more than three months before being allowed to finish her recuperation in an outdoor enclosure with ten other possums her age.

All of her wounds healed beautifully and were soon covered with lovely, soft, gray possum fur. She was left with a very slight limp from her fracture, but not enough to hinder her in the wild.

We knew she was ready to go outdoors on the day we attempted to completely examine our formerly docile patient and found her to be the possum from hell. She fought us long and hard and made the physical exam a complete nightmare for us.

Dog Bite stayed in the outdoor enclosure a little longer than her injuries warranted, due to one little mistake on our part: Juvenile possums are generally long and lean with a little pointy snout on one end and a lovely, long prehensile tail on the other. Dog Bite looked like a soccer ball with a tail. We had overfed her during her time in the medical center, and she had to slim down before release. After about four weeks of competing with ten other possums for food, not to mention the exercise of limb climbing in our possum enclosure, Dog Bite became a slim, trim version of her former self.

Michelle Lyons, Rick Over and Chuck placed her and her possum friends in carriers and carted them away to a nearby avocado grove. Dog Bite and friends casually ambled off, ready to face the world. With her appetite for life (and for food), we were sure she'd do quite well.

Avocado farmers in our area welcome possums in their groves, as they eat the rotted fruit that falls to the ground, as well as small rodents, carrion and garbage, thus keeping the groves clean and tidy.

As a matter of fact, friends Ben and Pandora Rose, on whose property we release many of our possums, have reported that their avocado groves have never been so clean since our last possum release. Way to go, Dog Bite! May your few short years on this earth be fruitful in more ways than one!

Our Golden Girl

One of Chuck's many projects in early 1992 was the construction of what he termed "a mountain lion enclosure." I
could never see the point, since neither we nor any of our
other area wildlife groups had ever rehabbed a mountain lion.
Prior to February 1993, Chuck had responded to two injured
lion calls—both hit by cars and both dead before Chuck could
reach the scene. This is pretty much the norm for lions hit by
cars, as tragic as it is.

My hindsight is so good. I know now that I should have
listened to Chuck when he said, "Build it and they will
come," in reference to this beautiful cougar enclosure. Always
in desperate need of enclosures, we weren't about to let this
beautiful pen remain empty while waiting for Chuck's lion to
check in. We quickly filled it with bobcats—five juveniles
came in as orphans in the spring of 1992 and were scheduled
for release in April 1993. This lovely enclosure gave them
plenty of space to grow strong, muscular and wild before their
release in the spring.

The whirlwind that engulfed us began calmly enough early
one Sunday morning in late February of 1993. The phone rang
and jolted us from our five a.m. newspaper and coffee routine.
It was the California Highway Patrol dispatcher reporting a
"hit-by-car mountain lion" on a freeway about thirty miles
from here.

The ever-optimistic Chuck gathered his gear and headed
for the scene. I stayed with the coffee and newspaper. I as-

sumed Chuck would be returning with another dead lion and saw no need to break my important morning ritual.

About twenty-five minutes after Chuck headed out, I received a call, this time from the San Diego County Sheriff's dispatcher. This "hit-by-car mountain lion" was now up and moving. I began to feel really nervous, as this cat was definitely not dead. I asked the dispatcher to have the on-scene deputies keep track of the cat, that Chuck would be there momentarily. My biggest concern was that the officers, not knowing what else to do, would shoot the lion. I contacted Chuck on the car phone; he was, in fact, almost at the scene. I prepared him for the scenario.

When Chuck arrived, he knew immediately where the lion was. The dispatcher who called me had obviously relayed my message to the personnel at the scene, as ten or twelve fully armed—and aiming—officers were lined up on the shoulder of the freeway, not taking their eyes off the brushy area below.

There she was—injured, addled from her accident, certainly not down but definitely in need of help. She obviously had a head injury and some road burns—this Chuck was able to note simply by observation. He also noted that in her confused state, she was pacing through the brush in a very methodical fashion.

He quickly formulated his plan and asked one of the armed officers to remain close by in case he was needed. Chuck's equipment consisted of no "state of the art" wild animal capture gear; all he had was an eight-foot pole syringe filled with about two and one-half ccs of a tranquilizer. Chuck

Because They Matter

was also equipped on that day with about 190 pounds of raw courage and a determination to help this injured lion.

As he watched her pace, he noted at which point she reversed herself to begin anew her methodical steps. This was her vulnerable time, the time when she was more concerned about turning herself around than she was about the humans watching her.

Chuck instructed his guardian deputy on the procedure to follow if his plan failed, and squatted as low to the ground as feasible as the lion made one more pass. As she made her turn, Chuck lunged with the pole syringe and gave a perfect shot to her left flank.

She spun around, growled, spit, lashed at the pole syringe, then began her methodical pacing as before. Chuck, who had coiled himself into a ball immediately after the flank shot, relaxed himself since he wasn't immediately attacked, relieved the attendant deputy of his duties and watched intently as the lioness' legs became rubbery while she continued her pacing.

After a few moments, she sought the sanctuary of the brush to sleep off the drugs and the bizarre events of this day. Chuck scrambled into the brush behind her to make sure she was all right and to verify that she was groggy enough to handle. On the hill above him, he heard a familiar voice say, "Nice kitty, Chuck."

Chuck, recovering from a massive adrenaline rush and wondering how he was going to get the lion from the brush below to the top of the hill, glanced over his shoulder to see the smiling face of Lieutenant Bob Turner of the California

Department of Fish and Game. Bob looked like "Dudley Do-Right to the rescue" to Chuck that morning as he helped Chuck carry the semiconscious lion up the embankment to our vehicle.

Bob held the lion's head while Chuck administered eye drops to prevent her eyes from becoming too dry. Chuck and Bob realized then that the lion was becoming a *l-i-t-t-l-e* bit too aware of her surroundings.

Since he had only lightly sedated her with the first shot, he gave her another little bit to ensure that she stayed groggy for the long trip home. It would have been an even longer trip home for Chuck had the lioness awakened midway through the journey!

After gathering his wits, getting the lion in the Trooper and heading home, Chuck called me, gave me some of the details and said he was returning with a real live lion. I began to have little panic attacks then. This was our first lion, and our mountain lion enclosure was filled with five feisty, juvenile bobcats that neither I nor any of our Sunday volunteers could safely move without the proper equipment, which was in the car, along with the mountain lion.

I quickly called Mr. Cool back on the car phone to make sure that he was all right and to tell him that I wasn't, and to ask him what to do. He calmly assured me that our old bobcat enclosure would be fine for the lion, not to worry.

Within a few minutes, Chuck pulled in the driveway followed by Bob Turner. I had never seen a live mountain lion and rushed to the Trooper to see her. Even sedated and with her legs restrained with nylon rope, she was the most exqui-

Because They Matter

site creature I had ever seen. She was long and golden and massive. I, for once, was speechless and had an irresistible urge to touch her—just once. Chuck, Bob and a few of our crew lifted her from our Trooper, placed her on the ground and began a physical exam. They checked her ribs, vital signs, road burns, teeth, eyes and sex. Four or five people were all over this cat, working quickly. I quietly stood back, waiting my turn to touch her.

After determining that the lion had a severe concussion and some road scrapes, Chuck administered an anti-inflammatory drug and antibiotics by injection. The lion was now ready to be put in her enclosure. I knew I'd never have another chance, so as Bob and Chuck were giving her one more once-over, I reached out to touch her power. As I did so (and I was almost there!) Bob said, "Here you go," and promptly handed me five ticks he had pulled from her body. I quickly disposed of them, but I had missed my one and only chance to touch her.

Chuck and Bob carried her to her temporary home, which we had already fixed up for her with a large shelter, water tub and plenty of climbing and scratching logs. We knew that once she came out of the anesthesia, injections to help her overcome her concussion and prevent infection would be out of the question. We'd have to slip pills into her food and hope that she would eat.

We have a three-day waiting period for injured, but not malnourished, adult predators. We have found that they generally will not eat for the first three days of their time with us, probably for two reasons: Predators do not eat every day in the wild; and the stress of being in a strange, captive environment can cause a loss of appetite.

In virtually all of the cases we've dealt with, by day four all is forgiven and the animal eats. So it was with our lioness. On day one we served her a beef roast stuffed with her medication. She didn't eat. On day two we served another beef roast and half a chicken, again medicated. Again, she didn't eat.

We had figured out an ingenious way of cleaning her enclosure without entering it, but our cleaning system could remove only small stuff, not roasts and chickens. Food was stockpiling. Fortunately, it was a chilly February, so we were not concerned about the food spoiling—we just wanted her to eat, take her medicine and eventually regain her freedom. On day three she got the hindquarters of a road-killed deer, medicated.

On the morning of day four, apparently all was forgiven—*all* the food was gone. Our golden girl was going to make it! The stress of necessary captivity had affected her but did not destroy her will to live. She continued to eat and take her medication every night thereafter for the nearly two weeks she spent with us, and was ready to be released.

Releasing a "rehabbed" mountain lion was new to us and to our local Department of Fish and Game. It had to be done by the book, if it could be done at all. I began to have little panic attacks all over again. This lioness was well and healthy and needed to go back home. What if Fish and Game in Sacramento nixed her release? If there had been any reports of lions preying on livestock or pets, or posing a threat to public

Because They Matter

safety within our lion's home range, we would not be allowed to release her. Our local Fish and Game officials, as eager to release her as we were, did a thorough check and found no indication of such situations within the lion's home range. She could go home.

We were all elated and began the preparations for her release. We pulled "Max" out of storage and got him cleaned up. Max is a huge, sturdy, stainless-steel cage that was donated to us years ago. The cage, with the word "Max" etched on the top, was obviously used to house a huge animal, most probably named Max. We don't know who the real Max was, and perhaps we don't want to know, but Max the cage has served us well.

Once Max was ready, with several of our staff, four Fish and Game officers and Dr. Don Wood, our veterinarian, in attendance, Chuck prepared the light tranquilizer necessary for us to prepare our golden girl for her trip back home. Once she was sedated, which was no easy task, Chuck and Dr. Wood weighed and measured her while Bob Turner attached a bright orange ear tag to her right ear. Again I was not allowed the pleasure of touching her, as I was in charge of videotaping the proceedings.

Dr. Wood's physical exam indicated that she was young, was not pregnant nor had she been. She weighed eighty pounds and was six feet long. Dr. Wood gave her a clean bill of health and helped load her into Max. The golden girl and Max were loaded into a Department of Fish and Game truck, and our entire entourage (except me) headed for the wilds of San Diego County.

The lioness was fully awake by the time they reached the release site. After a few false starts, the gate swung open and the lioness emerged from Max's belly. She was home. She ambled about for a few moments, turning only once to snarl and spit at those who had held her captive for nearly two weeks, then disappeared into the brush.

Eleven months later, her body, with the orange ear tag still intact, was found in the brush by the side of a busy road. She had again been hit by a car. Lieutenant Turner notified us of her death, and we were all deeply saddened. Our grief, however, was tempered by the fact that we had given her eleven months of life that she would not have otherwise had.

Our golden girl was a success story in many ways. Through the diligence of our local Fish and Game officials, we learned a great deal about our golden girl's habits and about mountain lions in general. For the eleven months after her release, what she did, or rather what she didn't do, was closely tracked by Fish and Game.

Any reported sightings of mountain lions within her home range were closely monitored. Although several citizens had reported mountain lion incidents, those citizens who saw the lions did not see a highly visible orange ear tag. This information was encouraging to us because of our concern that a lion that had been in captivity (although briefly) might lose its fear of humans. Our lion had not lost her aversion for humans and had continued on with her life—despite our interference —and had done quite well.

At her death, she weighed more than ninety pounds, gaining more than ten pounds in her remaining eleven months of life. Even in death, she was beautiful. We were thankful that the necropsy report indicated she died quickly from her injuries so that there was no prolonged suffering.

Our golden girl was an innately courageous wild animal with a spirit and a will to live that went far beyond our human comprehension, and this is meant to be her story. Yet her story of courage is no greater than Chuck's. His determination —and yes, his courage—gave "our lion" those extra months of life and gave us valuable insight into the behavior of these elusive, elegant cats.

Coati-Boy

Once in a while, an animal crosses our path and really doesn't belong here. We've taken in our share of domesticated ferrets that we've managed to get into the proper hands. We've also acquired a couple of caimans that we quickly got into better hands, as well as plenty of desert tortoises and various types of turtles that were turned over to our local turtle and tortoise society. The most unique, however, was the coatimondi who shared our lives for a while.

Our little valley was experiencing a pretty strong rainy winter storm when we got the call. State park rangers just north of us called to report "a raccoon—but not a raccoon" huddled in a tree fork as the cold storm raged. We called Cindy Mushet-Rogers, friend and fellow rehabber, to see if she could scope out the situation, as she was closer than we were. A raccoon huddled in a tree is not unusual, it was the "not a raccoon" part that had us intrigued.

Cindy, upon arriving and discovering that it truly was "not a raccoon," called Chuck for help. Chuck gathered the necessary gear and drove the thirty miles to the park. Cindy quickly pointed out the frightened coatimondi in the tree.

Although finding a coatimondi, a non-native wild animal, looking down at him from his fork high in the trees was quite odd, Chuck's most endearing and tension-relieving sight in this whole escapade was the vision of tiny Cindy keeping vigil while sitting on a dead log and covered head to foot in a large brown trash bag. She looked like a California raisin—a drenched one at that. To this day, Chuck calls her our "raisin-ette."

Getting this coatimondi out of the tree would not be easy, as he was pretty high up, very nervous and not about to come down on his own. Chuck loaded his eight-foot pole syringe with a mild sedative while Cindy and the park rangers readied the net.

The plan was for Chuck to climb the tree until he was within the necessary eight-foot distance, tranquilize the coati and, once tranquilized, nudge him from the tree into the waiting net below.

Sometimes these perfect plans work out, and sometimes they don't. Mercifully enough, things went beautifully for Chuck, Cindy, the park rangers and the coati.

The coati arrived at our medical center, still groggy and wet. We gave him a quick exam, which showed nothing but mild dehydration; otherwise he was fine. We set him up in our hospital, then did some research.

We learned that coatimondis are in the raccoon family, native to South and Central America with a few now trickling into Texas and Arizona. Knowing this gave us insight into

Because They Matter

what to feed him and also let us know that he was probably someone's discarded "pet."

The park rangers had seen him cower in the tree for several days and at first thought he was a raccoon. Only when they saw his tail did they realize that he wasn't. This poor guy had spent a couple of really rough days.

Although medium brown to dark brown as opposed to the raccoon's grays and blacks, the coati does resemble a raccoon, with one exception: The coatimondi has an enormously long, furred tail. Coati-boy's tail was at least the length of the rest of his body. Weighing in at thirty-five to forty pounds, this was a large animal with a lovely tail.

We did not know how handleable he was—only time would tell. When he was fully out of the anesthesia, we offered him food and water, which he consumed with gusto. He growled when we attempted to touch him, so we decided he needed more time and we needed our fingers. We left him alone.

Eventually we put him outside in a nice enclosure with plenty of climbing things and a great shelter. As with many wild animals, Coati-boy preferred the highest part of the enclosure and spent all of his time on a ledge near the roof, which put him at eye level to all of us.

He ate everything we put out for him and would let us touch him through the chain link, but he shied away if we attempted more personal contact. Being a scavenger, our coati was easy to please as he liked everything. We quickly discovered that peanuts in the shell were a real hit, and he would snatch them from us as quickly as we passed them through the wire. Coati-boy was a charming client, but we knew we couldn't keep him forever. He was lonely and needed his own kind. He was neither wild nor tame, and we had some searching to do to locate the proper facility for him.

Our search took about a year. In all that time, we constantly sought sources of entertainment for him. Since he was in the raccoon family, we felt that we could most please him by providing a diversity of food. He remained "moderately amused" with our choices until someone discovered his penchant for honey-roasted peanuts. They brightened his meager little life, and we were careful in the amounts we gave him. He suffered no ill effects. He got his "honey roasteds" a couple of times a week and always consumed a nutritious dinner as well.

After our yearlong search, we located a wonderful facility in Texas run by a woman named Lyn Cuny. Lyn deals with releasable and nonreleasable coatimondis and was more than happy to accept Coati-boy. Our job was to find a trucker who was willing to take our coati on the long trip from California to Texas.

We contacted Jay Scannell, a young man who had very humanely and professionally delivered some of our wild goats and burros into the capable hands of Chris and Mary Byrne, managers of the Fund for Animals Black Beauty Ranch in Texas. Chris and Mary had located Lyn Cuny's place for us and were more than willing to be our intermediaries.

Jay agreed to take Coati-boy to Black Beauty, and from there, Chris and Mary would get him to Lyn. After a string of phone calls back and forth from us to Jay, the Byrnes and

Because They Matter

Lyn, everything was arranged. Then came the vet check and the health certificate, an ordeal that did not sit well with Coati-boy.

The big day arrived and we were ready; however, Coati-boy was not. He looked at his nice padded carrying cage and looked at us as if to say, "If you think I'm going in that thing, you're crazy." He resisted all attempts to get him in the cage, and we finally had to give in and sedate him.

Sedating an animal is always risky, and sedating one for a long journey without the benefit of medical care, should the need arise, had us worried for Coati-boy, but we had no alternative. We finally got him in the carrier and, just in passing, told Jay of his history, his habits, and his penchant for "honey roasteds." Jay and his relief driver, along with Coati-boy ensconced in the truck's sleeping cab, were soon headed nonstop for Texas. We worried until we heard that all had arrived safely.

When Jay returned to San Diego, he called to give us the details. Apparently as Coati-boy was coming out of his anesthesia, he began trembling from the cold. Jay gamely opened the carrier door and gave Coati-boy another blanket, which soothed him for a while.

Sometime later, Jay's truck developed some engine trouble, which caused a delay of several hours. Jay checked Coati-boy, who was trembling again, and he began to worry.

Remembering what we had told him about our coati's "little pleasures," Jay purchased a pack of honey-roasted peanuts to help soothe our little critter. Jay said that Coati-boy snatched the entire unopened package, retreated to the back of his carrier and thoroughly enjoyed the rest of his trip. The coati made it without a hitch into Chris and Mary's hands, then to Lyn's coati sanctuary, where he has friends and his own tree. It is here where he will spend the rest of his days.

This coati's story is not just about him—it typifies the lengths that kind people will go to help an animal in need. Everyone from Cindy, our "raisinette" who kept watch over him until Chuck arrived, our staff who made great efforts to keep him entertained, Jay the trucker who went out of his way to help, Chris and Mary who were equally concerned, and Lyn Cuny who was happy to give him a home—all of these people depict the commitment toward animals that makes us all a little more human.

The Night Cranks

My God," I thought, "this is the ugliest baby bird I've ever seen." He was all pinfeather wings and spindly, ugly little legs, both of which he waggled constantly when he was ready to eat. He was about eight inches high, had a long beak, a long neck and large bulging gold-and-black eyes. He was not a pretty sight.

About a week after we took him in, we acquired another one, slightly older, but just as "waggly" and, unfortunately, just as ugly. Every time I think about these two, I have memories of Steve Martin and Dan Ayckroyd and "the wild and crazy guys" routine they used to do on the old *Saturday Night Live* TV show.

At feeding time, these two would attempt to out-waggle each other to the max. They were eager eaters and were easily weaned onto their natural diet. They continued to be really ugly, and I adored them.

These little double uglies were black-crowned night herons. They were delightful clients during their entire stay with us and were released in midsummer.

At one point during their childhood, while they were still in the medical center, these two learned to vocalize, and quite well I might add—especially when they were ready to eat. The first time I heard their vocalization, I was alone in the medical center doing an evening feeding. From out of nowhere, this resounding guttural *"blaaaht"* resounded and jarred my senses. I assumed it was a badly injured animal going into death throes. I quickly checked all cages and found everyone to be fine.

"Blaaaht" again and louder this time. I peeked in at the "golden boys," and there they were—*"blaaahting"* their lungs out, begging for dinner. I was relieved to discover that it was them and not some animal in pain. However, I was dismayed by the fact that now that these two had discovered their vocal cords, some poor fool in the medical center was going to have to listen to this all day long.

Things were already so stressful for us in that baby season of 1994. We were taking in an average of 300 orphaned babies of all species each month. Many required incubators and intensive care, and all of them needed to eat every time their mouths opened. The last thing any of us needed was to listen to *"blaaaht"* all day long and watch these two wild and crazy guys do their routine every time we passed their cage. Well, we had to endure it, because even though they were eating on their own by now, they were still a bit too small to put in the outdoor aviary.

By no small coincidence, that baby season was the one in which I quickly realized that our well-trained staff was more than capable of taking care of all these babies. Longtime staffer Michelle Lyons and I decided that quiet, sweet Trish Fuchs, our newest staff member, could use a little self-confidence, so we gave Trish the onus of the medical center that spring. She was in charge. She arrived early, stayed late, coordinated formulas, feeding schedules and cleanup.

Michelle and I didn't desert Trish completely, however. We were always there for a.m. duty, which often lasted from

Because They Matter

sunrise to noon, and we were always available for any questions or unusual behaviors that Trish wasn't yet familiar with. We didn't really intend to saddle her with this horrific job, yet as soon as the night herons started their noisemaking, Michelle and I suddenly found other things that needed to be done immediately—*outside* the medical center.

Actually, it was only a two-week period from when our herons first discovered their voices until we were able to move them outdoors. It was a long two weeks for all of us but especially for Trish, who rarely left the medical center that spring.

Most of our baby birds had to eat every half hour, so by the time one feeding was done, it was almost time to start again. And all the while, the "blaaaht boys" were doing their routine.

Trish would often emerge from the medical center to take a quick break, and I would see her looking slightly pale with just a hint of a smile on her face. Trish has a pretty smile, but this one was different; it was the smile you often see on the face of someone who has long, meaningful conversations with no one. I could tell that the boys were really getting to her.

It was trial by fire for Trish that year. She's a strong young woman, and she emerged from the medical center at the end of baby season with an enormous amount of knowledge about our native species of wildlife. She kept her sanity despite the herons, and I still remember the joy on her face the morning we decided to move them outside!

Their aviary was on a central part of the property. This meant that no matter where we were on the property, we could hear them. Whether we were in the office, in the pastures or—and this was the best—trying to sleep after a hard day's work, we could hear them. I couldn't wait to release these two, as they were most vocal after sunset.

Because of the rudeness of the vocalizations, Chuck called them "night cranks." They sounded so cranky and cantankerous, yet in truth I think their noises meant either "please feed me" or "thank you for feeding me."

Regardless, we were all happy to release them in a lovely habitat several miles from here. They actually had become quite beautiful with their juvenile plumage and their pretty golden eyes. I really did fall in love with them, as they had such delightful, spunky personalities, and—what the hey—I wasn't in the medical center with them for twelve hours a day listening to their complaints about the room, the food or the service.

Just at sunset about two weeks after their release, Chuck and I were jarred by a resounding double *"blaaaht"* coming from the office roof. Sure enough, Dan and Steve were there,

Because They Matter

asking for "some food, please." The night cranks were back! Somehow they had found their way home.

Both of them looked strong, healthy and well fed. I think they just wanted a taste of "mom's home cooking" again. Chuck fed them, they *"blaaahted"* their gratitude, then left for parts unknown.

To this day, we still hear *"blaaaht"* at sunset or sometimes in the middle of the night every few weeks. Chuck will say, "The night cranks are here." One or both of them will eagerly eat what he provides, then leave us again. Kids these days—you can't live with them and you can't live without them.

Now that winter has arrived, the night cranks are gone for the most part, and the color has returned to Trish's face. I don't have the heart to tell her "They'll be back!" as the next baby season is always just around the corner.

The Brave Mother

Cleveland Amory, our boss, says
rabbits are the creatures that God forgot.

I wholeheartedly agree with him. We deal with hundreds of wild rabbits, mostly cottontails, at our center, and have had ample opportunities to observe them, both in the wild and as orphaned or injured ones in our care.

From the time they emerge from their warm, tenderly made nests as babies until the day they die (rarely of old age), their lives are spent in fear of, or running from, a predator. In the wild, their predators are raptors, coyotes and bobcats. In urbanized areas, their predators are domestic cats and dogs, automobiles and, the worst and most frightening of all, man.

The mortality rate for injured cottontails who come to our center is depressingly high. Even though they receive excellent and swift medical treatment, the stress of being handled and confined is just too much for them. The youngsters aren't quite as skittish as adults, but even those with very minor injuries, caused by cats or dogs, often succumb to the stress.

The severely injured female cottontail who came to our center one spring morning taught us all a lesson in bravery and the power of the maternal instinct. A neighbor in our area saw a cottontail attempt to dash across a busy street. The rabbit was hit head-on by an oncoming car but not killed. The kind lady turned her car around, gently placed the rabbit in a cardboard box with the intention of bringing her to our center.

As she was carrying the box to her car, the rabbit began

giving birth. Although premature, the babies were squirming and appeared healthy. Their rescuer quickly removed the sacs surrounding each baby and verified that all were breathing, then rushed them and their mother to us.

The mother rabbit had severe head injuries but no fractures or other obvious problems on the rest of her body. We quickly administered fluids, antibiotics and treated her for shock and brain inflammation. We were certainly prepared to care for her babies, yet we knew it was vitally important that these babies get some of their mother's precious milk first, to protect them from the diseases that often affect young mammals. Babies who don't nurse from their mothers don't receive the colostrum, the first milk, which contains the essential disease-preventing antibodies.

After treating mother rabbit, we placed her and her tiny babies in a dark secluded area and left them. Throughout the day, we checked periodically, and it appeared that mother was resting comfortably with her babies nestled to her belly. Our fondest hope was that this mother rabbit would recover from her injuries and be able to care for her babies. This was not to be; twenty-four hours later mama quietly passed away with five babies clinging to her breasts.

The fact that these babies had their mother at least for a few hours immensely increased their chances of survival. We took the five one-day-old babies and began hand-feeding them. Our "bunny formula" isn't as perfect as mother's milk, but it's as close as we can come. Three of the five babies thrived. The two tiniest lived only four days. Every day we had these remaining bunnies was so special.

Because They Matter

We were proud of mother bunny and proud of ourselves for helping them along. After what seemed like an eternity, our three little miracles were weaned, eating natural foods with a vengeance, acclimated to the outdoors and ready for release.

There was nothing remarkable about what we did for those baby cottontails. Caring for them is our job, albeit a wonderful job. We feed hundreds of little mouths on a daily basis. The remarkable part of this story was the tenacity with which that brave mother cottontail clung to life, although mortally wounded, to give her babies her "gift of life."

Crow

Crow is a raven. Crow is a raven that someone *thought* was a crow. Crow, the raven, had been in captivity for several years prior to coming to us. He had apparently been injured as a juvenile and taken to a wildlife center that deemed him non-releasable, due to the nature of his injuries. Because money talks, a prominent San Diegan had been able to acquire Crow as a "pet." Apparently Crow didn't want to be a pet and for several years resisted all attempts at making him one.

After much pleading from us, Crow was delivered here for rehab. A physical exam deemed him a perfectly healthy, able-bodied bird who should have gotten his freedom years ago. His only defect was a slightly bent left leg, maybe from an old, healed fracture, but it was nothing that should have deterred his release.

Crow's years in captivity had made him accustomed to humans, but he was not handleable and certainly not a pet. We kept him in a flight enclosure for a couple of months to acclimate him to our area and then release him.

He hung around as we knew he would, and frequented our employees' break area, waiting for something to drop that he could eat or steal. We couldn't approach him, yet he came close to us to pick up dropped snacks. We quickly discovered his affinity for corn chips and flour tortillas, and Michelle, being the person she is, made sure we always had some on hand.

Late that summer Spaz came along. She was a dippy-looking juvenile who came to us as a baby, was raised with other babies and was released that summer with the others. All those juveniles stuck together, generally staying on our property, for quite some time. Spaz was easily identifiable, as she had a goofy little cock to her head and an enormous cowlick of wrong-way feathers on her neck.

Crow did his thing all that year, and Spaz and friends did theirs—until the following February. It suddenly became "ooh-la-la" time for Crow, who apparently found Spaz's bewitching ways just too much. We humans were completely ignorant of these goings-on—raven romance is evidently a very private thing—until one day we noticed that Crow was not in the staff lounge as he usually was, and Spaz was gone too. We were moderately concerned and hoped that they were okay.

Michelle, who had been off that day, called to see if Crow was home. We told her he wasn't here and hadn't been here all day. "Oh, my God," she whispered in the phone. "This is him then." A raven had shown up at her house that morning, one who looked vaguely familiar and who had a fondness for flour tortillas. How Crow found Michelle's house will always remain a mystery. She lives about two miles from us as the raven flies. Had he spotted her car or had he seen her in her yard that day? We'll never know. To compound the mystery, Spaz was with Crow.

During that period, we'd see Crow every few days, and Michelle would see him at her house as well. His bandy leg and quirky vocalizations were dead giveaways. We never saw Spaz again, but Michelle did and, to this day, still does.

By late spring, Crow stopped coming to our place completely and spent all his time at Michelle's, and so did Spaz. One day after scattering some flour tortillas on her property, Michelle watched in awe as Crow adroitly picked up a thick stack of tortilla bits and flew to a nearby stand of trees. From the distance she heard a sound we all know all too well—the sound of baby ravens being fed. Crow was just as busy as he/ she could possibly be, shoving food into those babies!

Michelle called us immediately to relay this wonderful news. What made this doubly special to us is that imprinted wild birds generally will not mate, and these baby ravens wouldn't need our help because they were being well cared for.

Within a few weeks, Michelle had a gangly bunch of juvenile ravens standing on her fence, along with Crow and Spaz—all were waiting for some delectably stale flour tortillas to come their way. We do not know who is the mother of the bunch, since we don't know the sexes of Crow and Spaz. However, in the politically correct world in which we live, Crow and Spaz were P.C. all the way and shared in the parenting of their kids.

Later that year, Crow came back to us periodically and acted as though he had never left. Spaz stayed at Michelle's. Spring of the next year brought a rerun of the preceding year, with Crow disappearing from us for a while, then he and Spaz with a batch of "juvies" showing up on Michelle's fence that summer.

During winters, Crow spends a good bit of his time with us, periodically creating a little raven havoc just to make sure we don't forget him. Crow really likes cars, and this is why we think he may have followed Michelle's car home to find out where she lives. When he's not busy stealing and burying food, he's busy with vehicles. He'll perch on a roof or spend a few minutes gazing at himself upside-down while standing on a rear-view mirror—just general raven mischief.

On several occasions the little charmer has actually been evil, and we all eagerly await his romantic tryst in the spring so we can have a breather. Fortunately, Crow has done his evilness only to the vehicles of those of us who work here. He knows our cars. The sheer, and in my mind, unquestioned intelligence of the corvids—ravens in particular—never ceases to amaze me. Crow is not special in terms of his well-planned capers; the only thing that makes him different from other ravens is that he performs his deeds right in front of us. Unimprinted ravens exhibit the same behavior, they're just sneakier about it.

Ravens play, eat and bury things. That is it in a nutshell. Speaking of nutshells, one of the more fascinating things I've observed are ravens with walnuts. Although their beaks are strong, a walnut is a tough nut to crack, so the enterprising raven merely flies around with the nut until he spots a hard surface, generally a paved road or a sidewalk. From high in the sky he drops his morsel onto the hard surface, often repeatedly, until it shatters. We often see ravens and crows munching on walnuts in the middle of our busy road. Crow has done it too, but if he can get an easier snack he will.

Trish Fuchs drove an old clunker. It was ugly on the outside and had a missing window; the inside wasn't much better. Trish had some clothes, shoes, leftover junk-food wrappers, assorted animal-rescue equipment, a bag of corn chips and God knows what else stashed in her old hatchback. Crow knew exactly what was in her car that morning, and he knew exactly what he wanted. When we weren't looking, he jumped into Trish's car, snatched the Doritos and invited his friends.

By the time we got there, the bag was almost empty, and Crow plus six or seven wild ravens were arguing over the crumbs in the bag. Trish's "nutritious" lunch was gone. I gave her a bowl of soup instead, and she learned a quick lesson about ravens and about "our friend," the big plastic trash bag, which she securely taped in place of her missing window.

Margot Havlik's car, a favorite of Crow's, was not a clunker but had a defective sunroof, which Margot kept open since it didn't close securely. This sunroof and, in particular, its rubber molding became Crow's mission in life. His obvious goal was to remove it. What his plans were later, we didn't know. He spent most of his time working at it, with our shooing him away when we saw him.

He evidently returned in our absence and accomplished his goal. We know this because late one afternoon, Margot's sunroof blew off as she was headed down the freeway. There are many lessons we can learn from the raven. Margot learned one that day—she had her sunroof replaced and now keeps it closed.

The key in dealing with ravens is to stay one step ahead of them. The problem lies in knowing which way they are going to go, so you can stay that one step ahead. We don't leave things lying about, we've learned that much. Anything that weighs less than a raven will probably be stolen by one.

When Crow is in the meantime "summering" at Michelle's house, Michelle regularly finds raven "prizes" buried beneath the tree where Crow and Spaz make their nest. These prizes range from gopher skulls to quarters and everything in between—whatever that might be!

Crow really likes the "Official Fund for Animals" vehicle, our Isuzu Trooper, and spends a great deal of his time in it, on it or near it. Our four peacocks like it too, and they and Crow apparently have a time-share situation with our car. When the peacocks are not pretending to be enormous hood ornaments or using it as a porta-potty, the Trooper belongs to Crow. He knows the windshield wipers very well, and the rear-view mirror is a personal friend, as are the seat belts and the steering wheel. Crow stashes treasured food bits under the wiper blades.

Both Chuck and I have been caught in sudden downpours while driving and have turned on the wipers only to find the entire windshield smeared with bits of canned cat food or fettuccine Alfredo or anything else that Crow had intended to save for later.

Chuck insists on keeping the driver's window rolled down when the car is parked, otherwise it gets too hot inside. We generally don't keep anything valuable in the car, so we think it's cute when Crow jumps inside, plays with the seatbelts and rides the steering wheel as if he's at Belmont Park. One morning, however, Chuck had left several rolls of nickels in the passenger's seat, intending to use them later that day for video money. We don't have good television reception in our area, so videos are our only source of entertainment.

Not knowing about the coins, I let Crow do his thing in the car, intending to shoo him away after I'd had a few laughs at his antics. Before I could shoo him, he rapidly popped out of the car and jumped on the roof with what looked like a cigar firmly planted in his beak. I tried to get a closer look, but he merrily flew away with his new toy and disappeared for the rest of the day.

I told Chuck about Crow's new toy. He checked the car and, sure enough, it was a roll of nickels. We knew we'd never find them and figured they were strewn over the countryside. We considered alerting our local businesses to be on the lookout for a raven trying to spend stolen nickels, but sanity prevailed and we did nothing but laugh and kiss our nickels goodbye.

Three days later, Crow apparently began feeling guilty. He was very busy on our deck, but I thought nothing of it. As we headed inside that evening, something shiny in one of our potted plants caught my eye. I found nineteen  nickels and half a coin wrapper, all lightly buried. Chuck had previously found six loose nickels in the car from that roll.

Crow kept fifteen nickels for himself, and I have no doubt that he purchased either a Pez, or maybe a couple of Milky Ways, but most probably it was a bag of Doritos for him and the "other guys" to share. I put nothing past a raven, and this one probably even found several seats in San Diego Jack Murphy Stadium so he and his cronies could chow down on their Doritos and watch our San Diego Chargers attempt to inch their way to the playoffs one more time.

Pansy

Animal abuse occurs in many forms.

Almost on a daily basis we hear horror stories about dogs being beaten, cats being mutilated and various other cruel acts inflicted on domestic animals. Abuse of wildlife also occurs constantly. Wild animals are routinely trapped in steel-jaw traps and destroyed, trapped in live traps and relocated away from their established familiar areas and family units, and shot from the sky for sport.

I am not referring to only the legally hunted animals during hunting season, but the majestic birds of prey who get blown away by yahoos with twelve-gauge shotguns, or the sweet songbirds who are slaughtered and maimed by the "mini-yahoos," the ten-year-olds who have to try out that BB gun they got for Christmas.

Life is tough for our native wildlife and becoming tougher due to human encroachment. It never ceases to amaze me that we humans, with our air of superiority and dominion over other beings, are the only creatures who don't regulate our own numbers when times are tough. We continue to breed and produce more of us even when we can't feed ourselves, let alone one more human being.

Wildlife species control their numbers and regulate litter or clutch sizes depending on several factors, including population density and weather conditions. However, often due to our failure to control our numbers, the wildlife suffer when we encroach upon them by overdevelopment.

Skunks and opossums have become truly urbanized and exist comfortably in neighborhoods all over the country. When we receive "nuisance" wildlife calls, we can generally allay the caller's fears regarding possums. With a little education, people discover how truly wonderful, helpful and beneficial they are to a neighborhood, and the problem is solved.

Skunks, although equally beneficial to a neighborhood and so delightful to watch, often present a problem when trying to convince a homeowner to let them be. The problem with these little stinkers is, naturally, their little stinkers. When a skunk feels that it is in mortal danger, it can emit an odoriferous spray that most people and other wildlife find highly offensive.

Chuck and I, all of our staff and most of our volunteers have been sprayed during various skunk-rescue operations. It stings when it gets in your eyes and has a really nasty taste if you get sprayed in the mouth (ask any of us—we've had it all!).

The nice part about being sprayed by a skunk is that after a while, you don't smell yourself anymore, so you figure no one else can either. I always get to be first in line at our local market if I have to go shopping following a skunk mission. As a matter of fact, I usually get to be the only person in that line. The poor checkers who have known us for years and know what we do just smile and give me really fast service.

Volunteer Barbara Woodhill also reported extremely good service at her local 7-Eleven when she stopped by for a pack of gum to celebrate the culmination of two weeks of baby-skunk rescue work. Barbara also noted that several days later,

Because They Matter

the doors to the store were still propped open. Some people just don't understand or appreciate our work!

The bottom line in dealing with skunks and other wildlife who frequent our neighborhoods is that humans will have to learn to coexist because the wildlife will always be there. Removing one animal will just allow another one to move into that niche.

Pansy's story involves animal abuse in its most grotesque form. It all began with live-trapping two skunks. Pansy, her mate and several youngsters came to us through the joint efforts of the Drug Enforcement Agency and the California Department of Fish and Game.

In an effort to conceal the odors emitting from his methamphetamine lab, an enterprising young felon managed to live-trap two skunks—a male and a female. He let them breed and raise the offspring. Skunks are wonderful, devoted mothers, even under extremely adverse conditions. One by one, this guy tortured and killed generations of Pansy's babies, then hung their bodies in front of the air vent to his lab. Passersby would smell only the skunk and not the vile offerings from his "kitchen." This apparently went on for quite some time until the lowlife was arrested.

The thoughts of this precious mother skunk as she watched her babies being destroyed still disturbs me after several years. I know how devoted the mothers are and how joyful baby skunks can be, and I wish the worst for the human who did these evil acts to them.

Pansy, several of her youngsters and the male skunk arrived one afternoon after spending a lifetime in hell. We placed the whole family together in one of our spacious out-door enclosures. Most of our mammal enclosures have wire bottoms covered by at least six inches of dirt, plenty for those digging mammals to play in but secure to prevent possible escape.

Pansy, her mate and her surviving babies thought that our dirt was a gift from the gods. Having been kept in wire cages with no stimulation, dirt was better than sliced bread to this dear little family! They rolled, dug, tussled and generally had a great time the entire time they were with us. They loved the food we served, loved our accommodations, but after several weeks of acclimating them to the wild, it was time to set them free.

Pansy and her mate, so cruelly taken from the wild, and their teenage kids who had never tasted sweet freedom, eagerly scampered from their carriers that warm summer day, obviously thrilled to be away from the chains of inhumane captivity that had nearly destroyed them all.

Woody Wood Rat

Baby rodents are beautiful.

We've raised and released many of these so-called "low items on the food chain"—gophers, mice, rats and squirrels. We have found them to be delightful in their zest for life, spotlessly clean and marvelous creatures to know. At our center, we do not differentiate between the predator and prey species, nor do we "prefer" one species over another. We care for them all, and if a person cares enough to bring a nest of orphaned field mice or a baby gopher into our center for care, then we will care for it.

Obviously, the younger these babies are, the harder they are to raise. Newborn mice and gophers are so tiny, fragile and difficult to raise, but we try with each one, and some of them do make it.

The circumstances that caused this newborn wood rat to arrive at our center escape me—I just remember that he came in very young, eyes not yet open, and we didn't know what he was. He was cute and he was a rodent, that much we knew.

Wild rats conjure up evil images in people's minds, and we hadn't dealt with a baby one before. We just kept thinking that this was the largest baby mouse we'd ever had! We just couldn't believe something this tidy and handsome was a rat. As he grew and grew some more, we realized that Woody was a rat—a wood rat specifically.

He was weaned quickly, as they are very intelligent, and was soon eating his natural foods. We had him in a lovely "habitat" cage, and he grew very attached to a sturdy twig nest we had purchased for use with our baby birds. Long after he had outgrown this little nest that formerly housed his whole body, he would continue to squeeze in as many body parts as possible that would fit. Generally, Woody would have just his head in there, sometimes his rear end, but always something. I guess even baby rats need security blankets.

When he was old enough, Michelle and Trish went "habitat hunting." Their mission was to select just the right twigs and branches for Woody's cage so he could begin doing "wood rat things." My two "earth muffins" were meticulous in their twig choosing and equally meticulous in their placement of it in Woody's cage. They were attempting to be wood rat mothers in making a comfortable home for baby Woody.

They did soon learn, however, that Woody had his own ideas for redecorating. After a few days of Woody trying to live with Michelle and Trish's tacky taste in decor, he decided to do it himself one night. We entered the medical center one morning to find Woody's cage completely redone. Woody had moved each and every twig and branch to the opposite corner of his cage. Some twigs had been strategically gnawed, others had been left alone, but each twig had been painstakingly positioned to make a lovely wood rat home. It was very reminiscent of my days as an elementary school teacher when I'd provide my students with tons of toothpicks and a quart of Elmer's glue and have them build castles for arts and crafts.

Michelle and Trish actually had done a pretty good job for Woody, but they apparently missed a couple of details that

Because They Matter

were important to him. First, they placed the twigs too close to Woody's toilet. He liked to sleep in one area and potty in another. I can understand that, I'm also that way. Second, they had neglected to place Woody's "security nest" within his castle. They obviously had not realized the importance of this item to Woody's well-being.

That night, Woody must have been extremely busy, redoing everything and probably muttering to himself about "those ignorant humans, just because they have thumbs they think they know everything." Woody had placed his house where he wanted it and had his twig nest securely tucked inside.

We were duly impressed and hated to disturb this masterpiece in architectural design just to clean his cage every morning. We decided to thoroughly clean it every few days, giving him fresh food and water daily without disturbing his habitat. Woody agreed to this and seemed content. Our friend Roberta Nau, who loves everything with fur, feathers or green leaves, knows a little something about almost everything. (Even if she doesn't, she hoofs it pretty well.) Knowing that Roberta has wood rats on her property, we asked her what she knew about them from her personal observations.

The best she could come up with on such short notice was that she had heard that if you left them a shiny gift they would take it and leave something of theirs in its place. Of course, being educated people, we didn't believe this for a minute. That doesn't mean we didn't try it though.

Michelle hastily produced a shiny bottle cap and placed it at the entrance to Woody's house one evening. The next morning we rushed to the medical center to see what Woody had done. Sure enough, Woody had taken the bottle cap, but in our haste to give Woody our gift, we forgot to notice what items of Woody's were already in the vicinity of the shiny cap when we placed it there.

We also did not know what items Woody would deem suitable for gift-giving. Had that peanut been there the night before, or that lovely plum tree twig? What about this dead leaf? I don't know what we expected—it's not like Woody could go shopping for us. He had limited assets—maybe we did get a gift and just didn't know it. We didn't play that game any more, as we knew we'd never know, and we were too embarrassed to ask Roberta just what type of gift we might expect.

We left Woody alone, cleaned his cage every three or four days and let him grow into juvenile wood-rathood without too much interference. Generally he was kind of groggy when we changed his cage in the morning, so we tried not to disturb him.

One morning, however, he was out and about, so we just sat for a few moments and watched this handsome, now-juvenile rat. As we were watching Woody, we noticed that he seemed to be relatively slow moving, not at all like the "busy beaver" we knew. Upon close observation we realized that one of his rear legs was injured. We pulled him out for an exam and found a simple fracture in his left rear femur. Poor little Woody had a broken leg.

We were extremely distraught, as it was almost time to release him. This injury would either completely nix his chances for release or, at best, set him back several weeks.

Because They Matter

We could only hope for the best as we couldn't set the leg; Mother Nature just had to take over and do her best on this one. As a precaution, we started Woody on oral antibiotics and moved him from his small cage into a large glass aquarium.

Woody did fine in his new home, as it had all of his old furnishings, including his nest and his bottle cap. It was sad, though, to see this active little youngster limping around as he rearranged his home. At least he still had the spunk to do his normal routine, albeit slower than before.

Within two weeks, Woody's limp was barely perceptible, and he no longer needed his antibiotics. He was basically back to normal, and it was time to set him free. We again turned to our friend Cindy Mushet-Rogers for help with Woody. Cindy has graciously accepted many of our "less-than-perfect" wild ones for release on her property.

Under Cindy's watchful eyes, many of our moderately handicapped but still functional creatures have been able to enjoy the wild side of life without ever knowing that someone is close by, keeping an eye out should they need help. Cindy, who knows every inch of her many acres of land, also knows just which animals inhabit which portions of her property, so of course she knew where the wood rats kept themselves.

Late one afternoon, Cindy stopped by to collect Woody and his belongings. She kept him confined for a few days prior to his release, then one morning she placed this handsome young rat in an abandoned wood-rat home along with his twig nest and his bottle cap—his memories of us, I'd like to think.

Cindy has not seen Woody since she set him free, but has informed us that the abandoned home in which she placed Woody now looks like some structure found in *Architectural Digest*; and ensconced in the middle of this lovely habitat are a tiny twig nest and a shiny bottle cap.

Blacky Raccoon

Of all the orphaned wildlife we deal with here, baby raccoons are among the most difficult to raise. The difficulty does not lie with the raccoons themselves, as they are quite easy to bottle-feed; the problem generally lies with the people who find the orphans. Rarely have we taken in an orphaned raccoon that hadn't been cared for by someone for a few days (or even weeks or months) prior to coming to our center. People find the babies irresistible, and everybody knows somebody who had one as a pet. By the time we get the babies, they are either very tame or very malnourished, small for their age and often suffering from massive diarrhea because of an improper diet.

Blacky Raccoon came to us at about three months of age and was suffering from all of the above. He was almost completely black, tiny and wiry, and arrived draped around some woman's neck. I knew we were in trouble with this one. Personally, I find it disgusting that with millions of domestic dogs and cats dying in shelters because there aren't enough homes for them, a person attempts to make a pet out of a wild animal.

Baby raccoons are, without a doubt, the dearest and cutest of all our babies. They require an enormous amount of care, since they are very slow to develop. Their eyes open at about three weeks of age, while other mammal babies open their eyes at ten to fourteen days. Other mammals are basically weaned at four to five weeks of age, but with raccoons, it's at least eight weeks. Consequently, they are handled more and, being extremely intelligent, they truly appreciate and bond with the "food person," whoever it might be.

Even adult "urbanized" raccoons in the wild will often develop a relationship with someone who puts food out for them (a practice we highly disapprove of, as it always leads to problems in suburban areas). Even we as wildlife rehabilitators frequently have to stop ourselves from cuddling these adorable little animals who need us so desperately. Too often we have seen the tragic results from improperly hand-raised raccoons. We strive to raise them wild and always with the companionship of their own kind.

Had Blacky stayed with the family who raised him, the following may have and, in some cases, certainly would have occurred: He very possibly would have died at an early age due to malnutrition (he was well on his way when he came to us), internal parasites, coccidiosis or salmonella (intestinal infections that are zoonotic—transmittable to humans).

Veterinarians in California often will not deal with native wildlife kept as pets because of the legalities involved in doing so and because of their lack of knowledge in the field of wildlife medicine, making diagnosis and treatment of an illness difficult. Only when a family member became ill and was diagnosed with one of the zoonotic diseases would the cause be discovered, probably too late for the raccoon.

Had the pet raccoon made it to adulthood, he probably would have had the run of the house (because he's so cute) and would have slept with one of the kids. Raccoons reach sexual maturity at about two years of age. Both male and female raccoons become quite aggressive upon realizing their sexuality.

Blacky would most probably have bitten a family member in his sexual frustration. At this point, he would have either been abandoned with no survival skills (a death sentence in itself), euthanized, or relegated to a small cage for the rest of his life. Or maybe at this point the people who raised him would have contacted us or another wildlife rehabilitation center. When raccoons reach that age and that state of maturity in irresponsible hands, the best we can hope for is to find a facility that can use a raccoon as an educational animal, as it is far too late for rehabilitation and release into the wild. The only other option is euthanasia.

To carry this scenario one step further, let's assume that Blacky's "humans" decided to put him in a cage. Blacky, being an extremely intelligent being, figured out a way to escape from his cage and wreaked havoc in the neighborhood and finally had to be put to death.

These are situations we deal with on a daily basis, especially with raccoons, because of their very nature as babies. None of these situations is right, acceptable or fair to a wild animal.

Fortunately for Blacky, he came to the right place at the right time. After a fecal exam, blood work and quarantine period deemed him healthy (although malnourished), Blacky was placed with five other juvenile raccoons in an outdoor enclosure. He screamed a lot at first and held on to the chain link like a prisoner on death row. He even managed to escape (only once) by squeezing between our legs as we were entering his enclosure, at which point he ran screaming to the first human he saw, climbed up volunteer Erin Keyser's body and nestled in her hair. Bright girl that she is, Erin gently lifted Blacky from her body and placed him back home.

We quickly secured the enclosure to prevent future incidents. I say quickly because the entire time we were doing repair work, Blacky was screaming and rattling the chain link like a neurotic monkey in a bad zoo. He did not know or like his roommates and wanted a human. This behavior continued for several days, which seemed like years to us. He was miserable and we were very concerned for him. After about a week, Blacky did settle down and actually began playing with the other juveniles and didn't scream for us nearly as often.

After several months and eight more raccoons later, part of our "herd" of fourteen was ready for release. We try to keep siblings and friends together when we release them so they can help each other out when times are tough. Blacky was among this first group, along with a little buddy of his.

This first group was crated up and taken to a wonderful raccoon habitat. We excitedly opened the carriers, and six juveniles scampered out simultaneously, ready for this lovely new world. The seventh refused to leave the carrier and had to be shaken out quickly enough to join his friends. It was Blacky, who ran a few feet away from the carrier with a wild look in his eyes. He then turned and ran frantically back toward his carrier, screaming when he was unable to reenter it. Seeing his agony and fear, we quickly opened the door and let him enter. He promptly vomited and had diarrhea, then calmed down.

Because They Matter

We were very confused, since Blacky had seemed so "rehabilitated" and ready to gain his freedom. We dejectedly brought him back home with all of our seemingly successful efforts in serious doubt. What were we going to do with this little midget who had so many strikes against him? We thought we had done our best.

When we arrived home, we put Blacky back in his enclosure with the remaining seven juveniles, at which time he ran toward one of the remaining older juveniles, a relative newcomer still recovering from minor injuries but well enough to be outdoors. Blacky had apparently bonded with this juvenile, more so than with the raccoon we thought was his "best bud."

In retrospect, this older, injured juvenile, who came in from the wild, was very people-shy. On those occasions when we were observing raccoon relationships, this kid was nowhere around. Apparently he and Blacky had kept their relationship away from human eyes. This timid little teenager was a great influence on Blacky, and within a month, Blacky, "The Kid" and the other six young raccoons were ready for freedom.

As a matter of fact, due to Blacky's small size and wiriness, he became the champion crawdad catcher of all the raccoons. We knew he'd do well at the chosen release site, an area with a pond replete with crawdads and assorted other raccoon delicacies.

Like an instant replay of several weeks prior, we boxed up the remaining eight raccoons. It was getting pretty late into the season for releasing raccoons. As Chuck would say, "We are rapidly losing our window of opportunity." What that meant for Blacky was that if he didn't go this time, we'd have him for another year, and then his chances for freedom would have become even slimmer due to the extended period of reliance on humans for food.

At the release site, we placed the four carriers in a row and simultaneously opened all four doors. Seven raccoons took off in leaps and bounds, hiding under logs, climbing trees and being normal raccoons. The eighth, Blacky, emerged slowly, then ran down the pond bank under the cover of thick vegetation—and began screaming.

The same thought rushed through all of us at the same time: "This is not going to work—*again*." We all had visions of boxing up Blacky, taking him back to our facility, admitting defeat and searching for a center that needed an "educational raccoon."

At the very moment that these thoughts were vivid in our minds, The Kid, Blacky's teenage friend, came out of nowhere, scampered past us and headed for the pond bank, straight for Blacky. In one of the most touching scenes we've ever witnessed, with Blacky's screams growing increasingly louder, The Kid began screaming, too.

They finally located one another in the brush, threw their arms around each other, screaming all the while. They both tumbled down the pond bank entwined in each other, stopped rolling at the edge of the water and stopped screaming. I swear to God, they were holding hands and smiling as they merrily trotted away from us.

We never saw them again. We returned to the site on the following day, just in case. We found nothing except ten

Because They Matter

million raccoon tracks at the pond's edge, and an equal number of crawdad shells as well. Blacky was probably demonstrating his prowess for the neighborhood raccoons.

To the best of our knowledge, Blacky's story turned out well. We have no reason to think any differently. It was a long, hard road for us and even worse for him. He was a confused, upset little baby when we took him in, another one of those sad creatures torn between two worlds—the wild and the tame.

Blacky's story is not unique among wildlife rehabbers, as we all deal with situations like this every year. Michelle, Chuck and I (the old-timers) find ourselves watching new staff and volunteers with eagle eyes when it comes to baby raccoons. If someone takes a little too long to feed them or cuddles them during feeding time, we begin having flashbacks to those terrible Blacky days.

Knowing that this new person is only doing what he or she is doing because of love for the animals and a misguided maternal instinct, we gently nudge this kind person in the direction of the baby sparrows or the baby barn owls. These two species rarely tame and will put any attempts at "coochie-cooing" to a screeching halt. Their attitude toward any human "food person" is "gimme the food and get outta my face." So different from Blacky and all the other raccoon babies, yet good disciplinarians for the potential bunny huggers—or raccoon huggers, whatever the case may be.

We humans have an urge to love and be loved. We have each other and our domesticated animals for that very reason. We all owe a responsibility to our native wildlife to love them enough to let them be free, to let them enjoy their true life-styles as we enjoy ours, and should these two worlds collide, we humans should not force our way of life onto these innately wild and "lovely for their wildness" other beings.

From Grrr to Grover—
A Tale of Two Possums

Grrr and Grover came to us at about the same time in September of 1994. Their time of arrival at our center was the only thing they had in common. We received a call from an area veterinarian who had taken in a young opossum that someone had found and brought into her clinic. There were no apparent injuries on this youngster, according to the vet, but he was just too young to be away from his mom. His body was about ten inches long, a definite juvenile.

We release juvenile opossums when they are ten to twelve inches long (excluding tail length), so we assumed that this youngster just needed a few days of good food and the companionship of other opossums prior to being released in a suitable habitat.

Staffer Margot Havlik volunteered to pick up this little "opie" from the veterinarian on her way home from work, house him overnight, then bring him to our center the next morning when she came to work. Margot had dealt with several possums here, so we were confident she could handle this "juvie." She left with her gloves and a carrier so she was completely prepared, she thought.

Margot successfully accomplished her mission and called me when she got home with the possum.

"Cindy, this guy is a little butt," she told me. "I had problems transferring him to the carrier."

I knew that older juveniles could be pretty aggressive, so I told Margot to wear protective gloves when she put food and water in his carrier. She assured me that she would, as the youngster had growled and lunged at her every time he sensed her presence. "Just be careful," I said, "and get him here safe and sound tomorrow morning." She assured me she would.

The next morning rolled around all too quickly, as it usually does. Margot arrived early with "Grrr," as she called him. When I got to the medical center, Margot informed me that she had put "Grrr" in with seven other just-weaned babies in the "possum condo." I expressed concern that this aggressive juvenile was much too large to be in with our kids. Margot assured me that this was not the case and pointed to Grrr in the condo.

As she pointed him out, this four-inch-long possum bared his teeth, growled (hence the name Grrr) and jumped at Margot's pointing finger. Grrr was, in fact, smaller than our other kids, but I knew he could hold his own. We were obviously misinformed about his size but speculated that because he was such an aggressive little critter, the veterinarian who called us saw him as much larger than he really was. I know I did the first morning I had to clean his cage!

Our possum condo consists of two levels of wire caging; a downstairs with logs and branches leads to the upper level. This allows the babies to learn some climbing skills before being put in the large outdoor "possum hotel."

To clean the condo, it is generally easier to remove everything—bedding, habitat, food and water dishes *and* possums. This was my plan that day. I removed all the inanimate ob-

Because They Matter

jects first, then the possums, one at a time. Picking them up by their tails is the safest way, so I gingerly removed our seven original, groggy possums and temporarily relocated them. They were a breeze. I didn't use my gloves as they are too thick to securely grasp the young possums' tails.

Everything went smoothly until I got to Grrr. Ungloved, I tried to grasp his tail, at which point he made repeated lunges and evil noises at my bare hands. He had made it perfectly clear that he was having nothing to do with me or my foolish plans. I had to get him out. His sleeping area was filthy, and I had to prove my superiority to three new staff members! I knew bare hands wouldn't cut it and neither would my gloves, as the little fool could slip right through them.

In desperation I grabbed a large sheet, quadruply folded, and tossed it over this little monster. I grasped Grrr and the sheet and temporarily relocated them both. I knew I had impressed our new staff members with my ingenuity, but I was worried about my next step: how to get him out of that sheet and into his clean condo.

Grrr went to sleep that morning, swathed in a huge folded sheet that would have covered his enclosure and three more to boot. What the heck, I kept all my fingers, our new staff members remained impressed by my abilities at handling vicious wild animals, and Grrr was very content. At this point I decided that our staff members needed the experience of Grrr; consequently, I haven't cleaned the possum condo since! Grrr reminded me of a tough young hood who, despite his bravado, still needed his mother. He was orphaned much too young, but with his tenacity, he would do just fine.

Because They Matter   207

Grover came to us from the California Department of Fish and Game as a result of a major sting operation involving the trade of illegal reptiles. Although not a reptile, there was old Grover peacefully napping as our Fish and Game officers confiscated more than 700 illegally captured snakes, lizards and whatevers.

The reptiles went somewhere, and we got Grover. Volunteers Stan and Cheryll Brown accepted custody of him, on our behalf, from Fish and Game officials; he is listed as "evidence" on the receipt. If all the wildlife we dealt with came right from the wild—either ill, injured or orphaned—our job would be so much easier. But nooooo, every few months we take in an animal who was supposed to be wild but became someone's "pet" instead. These always throw us for a loop. In some cases, if the animal hasn't become too confused, it can be rehabilitated and released. Old Grover was not one of those cases.

Possums don't have very long life spans, and it was hard to tell Grover's age, but we suspected he was less than a year old. He was more or less full grown but not yet having the enormous bulk that we see in older male possums. We set him up in the medical center and gave him all the comforts of home. He used a litter box meticulously and loved to snuggle deep inside a blanket or comforter.

We were very tentative in our first dealings with Grover, as we had never dealt with a "pet possum" before. We'd reach over to scratch him and be greeted by the old open-mouth possum threat. Though dealing with wild possums is scary, Grover's threat quickly turned into a yawn. He'd close his

Because They Matter

eyes and wait for a stimulating "butt noogie" or a relaxing behind-the-ear scratch. Grover was definitely too far gone for rehabilitation.

He also had stitches that needed to be removed as he had recently been castrated. That really nixed his chances for rehabilitation.

Staff and volunteers loved Grover—he was a pleasant, easygoing kind of a guy who would take grapes from our fingers. He slept most of the day and ate and used his litter box in the evening. Possums are nocturnal so we didn't get to see Grover's evening activities. Did he have little solitary parties and cavort all by himself? Did he ever think of the life he had or the one he could have had before humans interfered? I can't answer these questions, and Grover probably doesn't even ask them.

Possums are generally solitary and nomadic except during their breeding season, yet they have the freedom of choice when they are in the wild. Grover lost all of his freedoms of

choice when irresponsible humans came into the picture. We did the best we could for him and made his altered life as pleasant as possible.

So distinctly different were Grrr and Grover. Grrr will know the pleasures and thrills of living in the wild world—romping through the avocado trees, chasing bugs and rodents, munching on overripe avocados and chasing those lovely lady possums when he becomes of age.

Grover will have a nice enclosure, a little human companionship if he wants it, and some possum pals if he's the amiable sort. I can't help but think that somewhere in Grover's possum brain, he longs for the "other life." Instead, he's just listed as evidence in some police book somewhere and will spend his life in captivity, while Grrr will live to tell his grandpossums about the times he scared the pants off a dozen human beings who were nearly a thousand times his size.

Ehan

While reading this book, you may wonder why so many of the animals written about did not make it back into the wild. The fact is that thousands more, not in this book, have been released from our center and are enjoying (we hope) the best that the wild world has to offer.

We are overjoyed at releasing wild mammals and birds, as that is our ultimate goal for all the wildlife that comes to us. Sadly enough, the ones that do not go back into the wild are the ones who teach us about others of their species. They are the ones who accept death with nobility or accept permanent captivity so that their own kind can have a healthy blood donor or just a friend who looks like them when placed, by necessity, in an alien environment surrounded by strange "other creatures."

Ehan was our first golden eagle. She was a baby when we took her in during the summer of 1991. She had been shot—blown from the sky. Just a fledgling, she had probably just left her parents' watchful eyes for the first time.

We were called by the U.S. Border Patrol, which had custody of the bird. Apparently, someone near the U.S.-Mexico border had found her and turned her over to the nearest authorities. Upon receiving the call early one Sunday morning, Chuck and volunteer Stan Brown drove to the border to retrieve the injured bird. The Border Patrol had placed her in one of their holding cells. I am sure that no more noble creature than this eagle had ever been held in that cell before.

When Chuck and Stan returned to the center with the eagle, we examined her and discovered the buckshot, some of it still imbedded in her feathers; only x-rays would show how much of it was inside of her. Her left wing was severely fractured at the humerus. We knew it would take some very creative orthopedics to restore her wing.

We made her comfortable that Sunday and rushed her to Dr. Don Wood's office early Monday for x-rays and, hopefully, surgery. From the x-rays, Dr. Wood and Chuck determined that there was a chance, though very small, that the wing could be repaired. We opted to try, as we all desperately wanted this baby to fly again.

After two separate surgeries and weeks of recuperation, our hopes were dashed. Not only would she never fly again, the wing would have to be amputated—it was a complete hindrance to her mobility.

She had adjusted well during her weeks in captivity, had a voracious appetite, never seemed to lose her will to live and didn't become stressed out as do so many raptors undergoing rehabilitation. Because of her spirit and because she was otherwise healthy and would serve as an excellent blood donor and companion to future eagles, we chose not to euthanize her.

In her years with us, she has served her species well. She has donated blood on several occasions. The eagles she has saved are free now with a little of her spirit within them.

An entire elementary school has adopted her as their symbol for protecting the environment. In a campaign spearheaded by Pat Ravin, a teacher at James Dukes Elementary

School here in Ramona, the schoolchildren learned about the value of eagles and other birds of prey and how they can take measures to save wildlife habitats and thus preserve our native wildlife.

The children named her Ehan, a Kumeyaay Indian word meaning "all that is good." A large painting of Ehan is proudly displayed at the school. Painted and do-nated to the school by artist Linda Kelly, the work clearly shows that Ehan is missing a wing. Any child at the school is happy to tell visitors the story of "their eagle" and all they learned from her.

Many of the golden eagles that come to our center are simply juveniles, uninjured but malnourished and too weak to fly. This is a direct result of loss of habitat. Eagles require a tremendous range, and as acres of it are bulldozed for development, their food supply and nesting sites become depleted.

The only consolation to be had for this tragic loss of habitat for all our wildlife is that many of today's children are learning how to protect the environment and how to share it with our native flora and fauna. If we continue to destroy wildlife habitat, we will continue to destroy wildlife. The large predators—the lions, eagles and hawks—will be the first to go.

We, as humans, have already basically destroyed the North American wolf population, a passing that is regretted by millions. If we continue at our current pace of development, and with disregard for habitat preservation, our wild predators will disappear, as will we humans, the mightiest predators of all.